Sherman Adams

Orangeland

A description of the topography, climate, soil, productions, resources, advantages, opportunities, prospects, and general characteristics of Orange County

Sherman Adams

Orangeland

A description of the topography, climate, soil, productions, resources, advantages, opportunities, prospects, and general characteristics of Orange County

ISBN/EAN: 9783743414785

Manufactured in Europe, USA, Canada, Australia, Japa

Cover: Foto ©ninafisch / pixelio.de

Manufactured and distributed by brebook publishing software (www.brebook.com)

Sherman Adams

Orangeland

TOPOGRAPHY, CLIMATE, SOIL, PRODUCTIONS, RESOURCES,
ADVANTAGES, OPPORTUNITIES, PROSPECTS,
AND GENERAL CHARACTERISTICS

OF

ORANGE COUNTY,

FLORIDA.

SHERMAN ADAMS, Editor.

1883-4.

ORLANDO, FLA.:
PRINTED BY MAHLON GORE,
ORANGE COUNTY REPORTER.

In response to a very urgent demand from all parts of the Union, and even from Europe, for full and reliable information with regard to the climate, soil, resources, capabilities, progress, and prospects of the section of country in the very heart of the Orange Belt known as Orange county, it was determined to issue a pamphlet giving as full and concise information as possible. With this purpose in view Mr. Sherman Adams, a life-long journalist and a well known newspaper and magazine writer, for the past two years a resident of this county, has devoted several months to the gathering of necessary data and the preparation of articles upon the varied topics, taking great pains to insure the accuracy and reliability of all his statements. At the regular meeting of the board, the first Monday in October, Mr. Adams read several sections of the same in our presence and we authorize its publication, as having met the approval of the Board and being well worthy the attention and confidence of all who may peruse its pages, he having restricted himself to a plain statement of facts with regard to the points upon which information is so earnestly sought. We, therefore, endorse it as the official statement with regard to Orange county.

      KING WYLLY,
      GEO. E. SAWYER,
      D. B. STEWART,
      J. H. CAMPBELL,
      A. S. CAMPBELL,
        Board of Co. Com'rs

Orlando, Fla., Oct. 1, 1883.

FLORIDA

Florida! A Florida home! What magic in the word. What a host of sweet poetic aspirations are aroused by the mention. A home in the land of the orange. A home where the gentle kisses of the balmy breezes impart health to the body and joy to the soul. A land where the odorous forests and the fragrance of countless delicious flowers make the soft, genial, and soothing atmosphere an unfailing reservoir of health, strength, and calm, tranquil content. A land that, compared with the cheerless rigors of a bleak, frozen northern winter, is indeed an Eden on earth. A land of sunshine and of health, where the cruel myrmidons of wasting disease are forced to loose their grasp and flee before the advancing banners of victorious health, strength and joy. Thousands, snatched, as it were, from the very jaws of death and the brink of the crumbling grave, gladly give voice to the new life by which they are inspired, and recount the benefits to be realized in Florida.

Those, too, who are full of health and abounding strength, find here opportunities for advancement such as are to be found in no other state of the Union, nor in any other part of the known world. There is but one Florida. But one Orange county. Though the streams roll down no golden sands, though mines of diamonds are not to be found in her hills or water courses, yet her delicious and incomparable climate, and the peculiar constituents of her soil, place abundant wealth within the grasp of all who will but reach forth and take it. The golden apples of the Hesperides charm, delight, and enrich. The thousand productions that nature presents with lavish hand have but to be utilized, and lo! they are transformed into illimitable wealth. This is indeed the land for happy, healthful homes, where care shall be a stranger and want shall never show his haggard face. Here every one can sit beneath the shade of his own vine and fig tree, with vegetables in abundance at his feet and fruits innumerable of the choicest varieties by his side. Verily, this is no overdrawn picture. It may seem poetical phantasy; but it is practical certainty.

ORANGE COUNTY, FLORIDA.

CIRCUIT COURT—Seventh Judicial Circuit.
    WILLIAM ARCHER COCKE, Judge.
    A. ST. CLAIR-ABRAMS, State Attorney.

COUNTY COMMISSIONERS—King Wylly, Geo. E. Sawyer, D. B. Stewart, J. H. Campbell, A. S. Campbell.
COUNTY JUDGE—J. D. Beggs, Orlando.
COUNTY CLERK—T. J. Shine, Orlando.
BOARD OF PUBLIC INSTRUCTION—W. Kilmer, Chairman; W. H. Holden, C. A. Boone, E. A. Wilson, J. J. Combs:
SUPERINTENEENT OF SCHOOLS—J. T. Beeks, Orlando.
COUNTY SURVEYOR—J. O. Fries, Orlando.
COUNTY ASSESSOR—J. M. Owens, Umatilla.
COUNTY COLLECTOR—A. M. Hyer, Orlando.
COUNTY TREASURER—C. W. Jacocks, Wilcox.
SHERIFF—T. W. Shine, Orlando.

NEWSPAPERS.

Orange County *Reporter*, Orlando;
    Mahlon Gore, Editor and Publisher.
Sanford *Journal*, Sanford;
    Dr. J. J. Harris, Editor and Publisher.
Tavares *Herald*, Tavares;
    A. St. Clair-Abrams, Editor and Publisher.
Semi-Tropical, Eustis;
    Geo. F. Miner, Editor and Publisher.
Altoona *Argus*, Altoona;
    E. H. Vogt, Editor; Thos. J. Hinson, Publisher.
Apopka *Citizen*, Apopka;
    Rev. F. A. Taylor, Editor and Publisher.
Bitter Sweet, Kissimme City;
    Will Wallace Harney, Editor and Publisher.

BUREAU OF FLORIDA INFORMATION;
    Sherman Adams, Orlando.

Orange County.

This far famed section of country, that is developing with such unprecedented rapidity, is situated near the center of the Florida peninsula in its narrowest part and is the heart of the orange belt, climate and soil combining to make its luscious fruit unsurpassed. It extends forty miles from east to west and occupies a little more than from the 28th to the 29th degrees of latitude. It is below the limit of destructive frosts and is not subject to severe thermometric changes, though there are sufficient alternations of temperature to prevent that feeling of lassitude experienced in some tropic countries, especially in the sea islands.

Its location seems to be neutral as regards tornadoes and cyclones, their paths lying miles to the north and south of its boundaries. It is in fact situated in the same zone as the great civilizations of antiquity, the birthplace of the human race and the supposed site of the Garden of Eden. Hence, migration to Orange county means a return to first principles and the securing of those climatic conditions and natural advantages that the Creator deemed essential to the well being of mankind in its earliest development.

Orange county embraces an area of 2,300 square miles, 1,440,000 acres and 65 Congressional townships. Its surface is the most varied of any section of the State and all grades and qualities of soil and varieties of surface are disposed in the most peculiar, varied, and intimate juxtaposition. Though containing few high hills, and no mountain ranges or sandy deserts, the most of the surface is high and rolling, it being the water-shed of this portion of the State, several of the largest rivers having their source within its boundaries. The celebrated St. Johns river forms its east line for about a hundred miles, and the famed Ocklawaha quite a distance at the northwest. Magnificent lakes help inclose it on all sides, diversify its area and give favorable advantages in the matter of navigation. Lake George to the northeast, Lakes Monroe, Jesup and Harney on the east, and to the west Lakes Griffin, Eustis, Dora, Beauclair, Sams, Apopka and Johns, all fine bodies of water. At the south, Big and Little Tohopkaliga and Conway. In the interior, dotting the country at short intervals, are a multitude of pure, clear water lakes of every conceivable size and form, and many of them are well known from the thriving settlements on their borders. Lake front building sites being in great demand, not because of their scarcity, but on account of their beauty and many advantages.

LANDS AND SOIL.

The most of the lands of Orange county are high and rolling, the soil a sandy loam, and covered with a fine growth of majestic pine with black jack oak on some of the ridges of lighter soil. Next in quantity come the flat woods lands, also covered with pine, with now and then a tract of bushy hard wood growth called scrub, and an occasional cypress swamp of less or greater extent. These are too level for rapid natural drainage and are underlaid with a bed of clay or hard pan a short distance from the surface, and hence after a heavy rain fall they are covered with water for days or weeks. Many of these can be readily utilized by drainage and made very valuable vegetable and fruit lands.

In various parts of the county are prairies, of greater or less extent, and along the St. Johns river are extensive savannas that are overflowed at high water but at other times furnish excellent grazing for cattle. There are, also, occasional tracts of scrub lands that, now esteemed but lightly, will doubtless be eventually utilized, as, with the exception of less apparent fertility of soil, they have the same general characteristics as the rolling high pine lands, and when fertilized produce the very finest quality of oranges.

Along the margins of lakes and streams are lands covered with dense growths of majestic hard wood trees, live oak, hickory, water oak, magnolia, gum, red and white bay, maple, ash, cedar, linden, cabbage palm, and numerous other varieties. These lands are called hammock, and are classed as high and low hammock. The high hammock is very much like the high pine land except that it possesses a deeper soil with a larger amount of vegetable mold and is covered with hard woods instead of yellow and pitch pine. The low hammocks are virtually swamps. They have a very deep, black soil composed of decayed vegetable matter and where susceptible of drainage are the most valuable lands for vegetable gardens. Both kinds of hammock are found at intervals, though mostly of limited extent; jutting out from the lakes are similiar lands called bays or bay heads.

CLIMATE.

A great, though not by any means the only attractive feature of Orange county is its delicious climate, the superior, if the equal, of which probably cannot be found elsewhere on the face of the habitable globe. Being situated in the narrowest part of the peninsula, here but ninety miles wide, it gets the full benefit of the semi-daily breezes from Ocean and Gulf, with their harshness extracted by filtration through balsamic pine forests for about thirty miles on either side. Occupying the highest part of the peninsula, with a beautifully rolling surface, and with no high mountains within many miles to deflect the natural air currents, with no extensive swamps or other sources of miasm to poison the air, its surface being mostly a sandy loam, covered with aromatic pine forests, it is evident that no locality can possibly possess more healthful conditions.

HEALTHFULNESS.

Experience proves that its healthful surface, its clear, sunny atmosphere thus tempered and medicated by live, healthful odors constantly renewed, its clear, pure water, its delicious fruits and choice vegetables, are not only conducive to health but curative of disease, and people can live and thrive here on a diet and under conditions of neglect and subject to exposures that would destroy them elsewhere. As an example of its effect on the physical system the native race of Indians may be cited. Nowhere did the Spaniards find such desperate, bitter, and successful resistance to their encroachments, cruelties and tyrannies as from the hardy, lithe, and finely proportioned Indians of the Florida peninsula, and nowhere has our own Government found the race more difficult to subdue. The very air is instinct with freedom from all that enthralls body and mind. Besides this, several of the most destructive diseases that afflict mankind and fill the world with sorrow and mourning are unable to maintain a foothold in Orange county. The virtues of the climate successfully defy their power and many a stricken sufferer has here found a city of refuge where he, or she, could safely hurl defiance at the fell destroyer. The diseases referred to are, Pneumonia, (very rare), Diptheria, (none), Typhoid Fever, (very rare), Phthisis, (very rare), Yellow Fever, (none), Hydrophobia, (none,) Sun Stroke, (none).

Orange county is in fact the "Sanitarium of the World," and year by year, as the virtues of her incomparable climate, the excellence of her location, the purity of her water supply, the varied character of her topography, the resources and excellent and productive qualities of her soil, its adaptability to almost every product of both the temperate and the tropic zones, the illimitable number of lovely and desirable locations for residences, the opportunities to engage in whatever occupation one may prefer, the ease of obtaining a livelihood and securing a competence or a fortune for declining years; all these and many other facts that might be adduced combine to account for the great esteem in which Orange county is held and are potent reasons for her rapid development.

MOST DEVELOPED LOCALITIES.

Although individuals have located here and there, all over the county, the great majority have made their homes in the lovely strip of country but a few miles wide that extends either side of the South Florida railroad from Sanford on the south side of Lake Munroe, the natural gateway of the county, to Orlando, the county seat, and a few miles beyond. Within the last two or three years and since the completion of the Astor & Lake Eustis railroad, the delightful high and rolling country in the northwestern part of the county, in what is known as the "Great Lake Region," is justly developing with unexampled rapidity. The completion of the extension of that road to Tavares to the south and of another branch to Leesburg in Sumpter county on the west and the completion of the standard guage road to Tavares, and of the Tavares, Orlando & Atlantic road, also a standard guage, to Orlando the present season, will aid immensely in the rapid development of the whole western portion of the county, which, being nowhere surpassed, only awaits ready transportation to become very thickly settled. The whole northern part of the county from Lake George to Lake Munroe has as yet attracted but few settlers, and the same is true of the whole southeastern and southern portion, excepting Kissimmee City on the South Florida railroad, which is growing rapidly. The opening up of numerous projected lines of railroad will hasten the growth of other sections, especially that very fine portion in the vicinity of Lakes Apopka, Stark, Butler, Wanee, etc. In fact, all over the county are beautiful lakes and choice locations, productive and desirable lands that now settled by families some distance apart only need to be known, and the daily visits of the iron horse, to speedily fill them with a prosperous and contented people surrounded by every comfort and with the means of gratifying every reasonable desire.

OWNERSHIP OF LANDS.

The lands throughout the county are mostly in the hands of individuals, and the day is past when many good Government homesteads can be located, though one can be found occasionally, and the relinquishment of others that are improved or partially improved, can now and then be purchased at a moderate price. There are, also, some lands held by the Disston company and by different railroad companies that are selling at reasonable rates. Land is plenty, however, for nearly every settler has several times as much as he can improve, a portion of which he prefers to sell that he may have more neighbors, and also secure means to improve the remainder. Here no one needs more than five acres, and he can get a better living from that amount and have a fatter pocketbook than from an average fifty acres at the north, or in other parts of the South, and do it more easily and with less anxiety.

PRODUCTS AND AVOCATIONS.

This is a fruit and vegetable and not a farming country, as the term is generally understood. A man does not revel in view of his broad acres and extensive fields of waving grain, but derives his satisfaction from his well tilled garden and beautiful, fruitful grove of luxuriant evergreen and its luscious golden fruit that assures him an independent income and prospects constantly brightening.

The generality of avocations may be followed here, but the first duty of every man is to secure a few acres of land and commence its improvement. If he has but little means he must go slow, work for his neighbors for his livelihood and develop his own land as he has opportunity. This will prove a savings bank to him and he can see his capital steadily increasing without fear that some speculative and dishonest bank president or cashier may squander his substance and reduce him to penury. In his fine groves of the varied fruits of the citrus family and his small yet well tilled field, he has the assurance of a comfortable provision for all future wants and a sure inheritance for his children and children's children after him to the third and fourth generation. What can prevent a man so situated from having a constant feast of calm and joyous content, for a quite small grove assures an independent income.

ADVANTAGES OFFERED.

Orange county offers great inducements to the man of means and to the man of little property. Everything here shows intense activity. Values are increasing rapidly and we have yet to learn of a single judicious investment that could not have been resold in a few weeks or months at largely enhanced prices. Now is the time to better your condition. "A word to the wise is sufficient."

HOW TO REACH ORANGE COUNTY.

The natural and customary gateway to Orange county is by St. Johns river steamers to Sanford on Lake Monroe, 200 miles south of Jacksonville, thence by the South Florida railroad to the various towns along its line to Kissimme City, forty miles to the southward. From the several stations conveyances can be had at reasonable prices to any point in the contiguous country.

The route for those wishing to go to the Great Lake Region in the northwest part of the county, is to leave the St. Johns river steamer at Astor and take passage on the cars of the St. Johns & Lake Eustis railroad to any desired locality. Conveyances can be had to visit the surrounding country.

Through trip tickets to Astor or Sanford can be secured at any of the principal offices in the North or West, by rail or water, or both combined.

A WORD OF ADVICE.

After reaching the objective point in the county, secure comfortable quarters and devote a few days to quiet observation and the making of acquaintances. Visit different sections and learn their special characteristics. Every locality has its specific differences and it will be well for you to acquaint yourself with them. Every place desires to secure new settlers, but you need time to learn which will suit you best. Some persons will disparage every location but their own. When you meet such an individual beware of him for he will try to deceive you. There is, however, one feature peculiar to Florida—every individual seems to really believe that there is no other locality equal to his own. This is strange, but true. Do not get excited and boast what you propose to do. Keep your eyes and ears intelligently open and incite your reflective faculties to their proper duty. Assure yourself that you know nothing whatever of the country or the conditions necessary to success. You will find very many things different from what you expected; not worse, but different. You will find the people quite as active, intelligent and cultured as those you have been accustomed to meet, and as honorable and straightforward in their dealings and representations, and they know much better than you do the country and its capabilities.

LOCATION, EXPENSE, ETC.

Having determined upon your location and assured

yourself that it is favorable to your contemplated business or avocation, the next thing to be done is to have a requisite portion cleared, fenced and made ready for the contemplated crop or grove. The expense will vary in different localities, but estimates will be given in succeeding pages.

A house is in order and that will cost whatever amount you may please, depending upon size and style, for all sizes, qualities and styles are in fashion. The log house period has passed, hence, you will probably, but not necessarily, build of boards. Rough lumber costs $14 to $16 per M; planed $18 to $22; shingles $4 to $6. There are numerous saw mills in the county, but more are needed to accommodate the rapidly increasing population.

PLANTING GROVES.

Groves are set out at all seasons of the year, the only requisite seeming to be that the ground be or be made moist for a few days. If the heavens fail to supply water you can cart (or "tote") it from a lake or well. The prices of young trees range from 25 cents upwards according to size. Nice ones are 75 cents to $1.00 each. You should get several varieties each of oranges, lemons, limes and guavas. Near the house yard you should also have grapes, figs, Japan plums, Japan persimmons, several kinds of mulberries, almond, olive, pomegranates, grape fruit, citron, date palm, paw-paw, mango, and a variety of other trees. Also pineapples, bananas, strawberries, pepper tree, palma christa, pecan, etc., etc. It will be but little trouble and will well repay you. The Japan persimmon and the mulberry grow very rapidly and make beautiful shade trees.

GARDEN VEGETABLES.

A good vegetable garden can be started at once and will do well with care, but the soil needs special preparation and fertilizing as there is an acidity in the soil that requires stirring and the sun's influence to remove. An application of lime would doubtless hasten the sweetening process. The safest crops for the first year are cow peas and sweet potatoes. Garden vegetables can be planted at almost any season of the year, and with proper care and fertilization produce excellent results. Hammock lands are preferred for gardens but the high pine lands with one-quarter the fertilization customary at the North, show great productiveness, the vegetables being of fine size and excellent quality.

WHAT TO DO AT FIRST.

An important question with many, and especially to those with limited means, is how to get along the several years required for their groves to come into bearing. The rich can busy themselves with improvements without regard to income, but the poor man and the man of limited means also desires the luxury of living in so unequalled and incomparable a climate, the merits of which the most enthusiastic writers are unable to but feebly describe. It must be experienced to be realized. Hence the frequent question, "What can I do for a livelihood the first few years?"

A man cannot put money in a savings bank or invest it in business unless he has it. What are you doing now to secure a livelihood? Working. Well, you can get a living and ought to save something besides, by working here. The cost of eatables here is just about the same as where you are. Here you save the expense of fuel to a great degree; also save largely in clothing. Besides, the inducements for and opportunities of spending money for mere personal gratification, to indulge some whim or passing fancy, are less here than there. Neither do people spend as much for style and they are not expected to. In short, you can and are expected to live more cheaply in every respect than in other sections of the country. You are laying the foundations of future competence and independence—of a fortune.

But, howsoever much you may save, something must be brought in to keep the larder filled and the pot boiling. What shall it be? The first recourse is manual or mental labor for others. Many have begun thus and succeeded. The next recourse is to raise something for yourself. Learn from your more intelligent neighbors what crops you can raise speedily and how and when to plant them. This embraces the whole range of vegetables, rice, corn, sugar cane, cotton and tobacco. A good income can be secured in two or three years by planting orange and other seeds and raising young trees for sale. Pine apples, also, yield a return the second year. Strawberries yield in a few months. If you know how to manage poultry successfully you can make them yield you a handsome income with little delay. Poultry do well here and pay excellent profits, besides improving the land on which they range.

What one can do depends mainly upon the individual and his previous habits and experience. Each one will increase his means according to his enterprise and ability. No one has been known to die of starvation here. There is work for all. Some can chop down trees or split rails, grub the roots out of new land, dig ditches, plow, plant, hoe, or help build houses. There is plenty of work for all and good wages. No one can afford to sit down and wait for his orange, lemon, or lime trees to come into bearing, for there is a long interval between the piney woods and the golden fruitage. Be up and doing with a heart for any fate and success is certain. There are fewer drones here than at the North. It is discreditable to have no earnest avocation.

WHAT PEOPLE ARE DOING.

As previously remarked orange growing is the predominant industry. Some are giving a part of their attention to limes, lemons, Japan persimmons, pine apples, strawberries, and other fruits ; some to raising vegetables and get quicker returns. There are a variety of kinds of business that can be carried on successfully. Human nature and human wants are the same here as elsewhere. The opportunities offered are many and the man of enterprise and intelligence will adapt himself to his circumstances and improve the chances offered. Many new manufactories might be started with profit to the individual and benefit to the community.

THE CLASS OF PEOPLE HERE.

The people here as a rule are the more intelligent and enterprising from all communities. They mean business and work accordingly. They are laying the foundations of future fortunes. Those who come here expecting to find an ignorant, shiftless, unambitious people will be greatly mistaken. In no section of the world will be found a more intelligent, earnest, orderly, and law-abiding class of citizens. They are making the wilderness blossom as the rose, and developing delightful homes in what is to be the wealthiest State of the Union. Many of their yards are filled with flowers and ornamental shrubs and trees that bloom throughout the year, and here the ladies can indulge their love for the beautiful to their hearts content and dwell amid the choicest flowers the year round.

KINDS OF LAND.

As before stated the lands are varied and every reasonable desire can be satisfied. There are seven grades of lands : High and low hammock, prairies, flat-woods, and the rolling, high pine lands that constitute the larger portion of the surface. There are occasional limited areas of scrub, and now and then a cypress swamp. There is very little of the surface but will prove available. The numerous clear-water lakes add greatly to Orange County's manifold attractions, and it is sure to be the most densely populated of any section of the Union, excepting the large cities, and there will be more true and lovely homes to the square mile than can be found elsewhere. It will be a land of hotels, boarding houses and happy homes surrounded by evergreen fruit trees and flowers, and plats of choice fruits and vegetables ready for use every month in the year.

FUTURE CONDITION.

Of large cities there will be but few, or none, but there will be a local center every two or three miles, if not even nearer, with school, church, postoffice, store, etc., and every family will be in comfortable or independent circumstances, for, from their plat of from two to five acres of well tilled land, they will derive an income of at least $500 to $1,000 per acre, and probably more, for they will adopt the intensive system of cultivation. Their houses will be well supplied with all the appliances of modern civilization, with books and works of art, the latest publications, and their necessary hours of labor will be so few that they will have abundant leisure to improve their minds by study and social converse. Relieved from the predisposing causes to care and worry, they will enjoy excellent health and be in a condition to secure their full share of all the joys that life affords. What can be more desirable or attractive?

Communication with different localities will be easy, for the whole section of country will be intersected and bisected by the many lines of railroads that will be required to transport the immense crops of fruit and vegetables that will be produced here. Probably no section of the Union will have so many miles of railroad to the square mile as will the Orange Belt of Florida. Then, too, numerous lines of steamers will traverse the many navigable lakes and rivers, and innumerable opportunities for enjoyment will be afforded both visitors and residents.

HEALTHFULNESS OF ORANGE COUNTY.

The prevalent diseases and the liability of being prostrated by sickness are very important factors in determining the desirability of any county, or section, as a place of residence, either temporarily or permanently. Of Orange county we feel confident that we can conscientiously assert that there is nowhere a section of country of equal size, with so great a variety of surface, soil, etc., that is as free from diseases of all kinds. People are sick more or less everywhere, and it is appointed unto all once to die, but here diseases are of a very mild type, usually yielding readily to treatment, and the few practicing physicians get but very little business from the resident population, their income being chiefly derived from invalids who come here for the benefit of their health, while statistics show the death rate to be less than in any other section of the Union, notwithstanding the thousands of invalids in every stage of disease who come here annually, as a last resort, in the hope of improving their health, and the great majority find health improved and life prolonged.

On the rolling, high pine lands there seems to be no prevalent disease whatever, though wrong habits, overeating, or overexertion may bring on an attack of indigestion or biliousness. In the low hammocks and wet, marshy places there is here as elsewhere a liability to billious and malarial fevers, but unlike thousands of other localities, they are of a mild instead of a virulent type, and by proper treatment the patient is soon restored to health. Of the great list of diseases so common at the North and West and the South we know nothing.

INSECTS, REPTILES, ETC.

The prevalent insects that here, as well as elsewhere, annoy mankind are mosquitoes, fleas, gnats and roaches. There are but very few house flies, strange as it may seem. A walk along the grassy margins of the lakes and streams while wet with dew will often insure a few minute insects called red bugs, that, if not removed, will burrow in the flesh and make a running sore, but a wash with plenty of soap usually disposes of them or, if they have burrowed in the skin before discovered, an application of kerosene and sulphur destroys them at once.

Mosquitoes are far less numerous in Orange county than in many other parts of the Union and are mostly confined to low localities, the low borders of bodies of water, etc. Very few infest the rolling high pine lands. For some unexplained reason fleas seem to cause but little trouble after the first year, but will breed on hogs and dogs. Gnats also infest but few localities, and in all our travels in the county we have found but one or two places where they were annoying and but few where we noticed their presence. Roaches are no more prevalent than in other southern and in many northern localities.

POISONOUS SNAKES

Are a great bugbear with many, but in constant travels over all kinds of land and at all hours both of day and night we have yet to see the first rattle snake, either dead or alive, and but two or three moccasins, and they were in so great hurry to get away that we did not have a chance to kill them. They only inhabit damp localities. Of all kinds of snakes there are far less than in Massachusetts or New York. Mr

J. O. Fries, the U. S. Deputy Surveyor, who has probably traveled in the past ten years more miles over the lands of Orange county than any other man, being constantly employed in surveying, tells us that in his travels over all kinds of lands he has seen but seven poisonous snakes. Probably no active surveyor in the North, West or South can say the same. The fact is there are very, very few snakes on the habitable lands of Orange county.

CHIEF PRODUCTS.

The great absorbing industry of Orange county is the growing of groves of orange and other citrus fruit trees, the lands and climate being peculiarly adapted to the production of these luscious fruits, the "golden apples of the Hesperides." Several thousands of acres have been cleared of their forest growths and set with orange trees and other citrus fruits and at the present rate of progress, but very few years will elapse before the entire available surface of the county will be covered with these stately evergreens, a broad expanse of bridal blossoms, or laden with millions and millions of the most delicious fruit that here attains its greatest perfection, nourished by the genial sun and unharmed by frost. Without exaggeration, or invidious discrimination, it may be justly said that Orange county is in a preeminent degree the especial home of the orange, and that no other section equals it in this regard, for it has within its boundaries every required condition of preeminently successful culture.

Why should orange growing be such a favorite pursuit? Because a few years of care and labor and a small investment secures to the possessor of even a small grove a sure support, a competence for himself and his children after him and their descendants for several generations. Because the care of a grove is one of the most pleasant and healthful of occupations. Little hard, severe, labor is required after the ground is once properly cleared and prepared, and yet there is sufficient to keep all the faculties of both mind and body in vigorous and harmonious activity.

We might give many examples of men who, with little or no money have raised groves that give them an ample support and are making them wealthy; of men of means who have secured fortunes. These are matters of history and orange culture is no longer an experiment but the chief business of Orange county.

Besides oranges, every man who secures one or more acres in this unequalled section will plant, for his own use at least, if not for market, lemons, limes, guavas, figs, bananas, grape fruit, shaddock, grape vines, Japan plums and persimmons, mulberry trees, apricots, citron, mango, paw-paw, sugar apple, pomegranate, olive, prune, almond, date palm, pecan, and numerous other fruits. In some parts the peach, pear, and apple may be successfully cultivated. Blackberries and huckleberries flourish. Every man should have a plat of pine apples, as they need but little if any protection. Also strawberries, as they yield largely, bearing from December to June a most luscious fruit.

Guavas are very prolific bearers, and as soon as canning factories become sufficiently numerous will be a source of great profit. They are now very extensively used by the residents, but are too perishable for present modes of shipment. With the completion of direct lines of railroad to the North, and the use of refrigerator cars, they can probably be shipped with great profit.

Pine Apples are a profitable crop on rich or well fertilized land, yielding at the rate of $500 to $1,000 per acre. They sometimes need a slight protection.

The Grape is cultivated with great success, both soil and climate being peculiarly adapted to the vine. Immense yields are reported.

The Palma Christa, or Castor Oil Bean, grows finely, speedily becoming a tree of large size and yielding heavily. The ground on which it is grown increases rapidly in fertility. It reaches twenty to thirty feet in height. It bears the first year.

The Banana, though sensitive to frost, is a very profitable crop, from one to two thousand dollars per acre income being claimed. It requires rich land, grows from ten to twenty feet high and bears in about eighteen months after setting. No family should fail to devote a good plat of land to this pleasant and nutritious fruit.

The Fig is readily propagated from cuttings and fruits the second or third year. It grows luxuriantly and requires but little care. It is wholesome and nutritious, rich and luscious and is generally much prized by children. The tree, or more properly bush, with cumbrous jointed limbs, grows to a considerable size and attains a great age.

The Lemon is considered about as profitable as the orange, but grows more bushy and does not make as handsome a tree. Quite a number of improved varieties are being grown.

The Lime, like the lemon and guava, is more sensitive to the cold than the orange, and grows as a large shrub or bush, branching at the ground from the main trunk. It is a very desirable and profitable fruit.

The Shaddock, with its half dozen varieties, one of which is the grape fruit, makes a tree resembling the orange and the stock is excellent for budding. The fruit is several times as large, with an acidulous, juicy, aromatic, and somewhat bitter pulp. It is very desirable for home use though not yet grown for market.

The Japan Plum and Persimmon are being introduced to a considerable extent and give great satisfaction, the fruit being excellent and the trees ornamental as well as useful.

The Mulberry is considerably cultivated and is one of the most satisfactory of trees, growing with remarkable rapidity, forming an excellent shade and yielding a pleasant and wholesome fruit resembling the blackberry. There are a number of varieties, several of which should be secured at once by the new comer. Under favorable circumstances they will attain a height of twenty or more feet the second year.

The foregoing are the more important fruits most extensively cultivated, but there are numerous others grown to a limited extent and deserving of extended and general culture. Every family should have a few of each kind for home use, as they would afford much satisfaction.

AGRICULTURAL PRODUCTS OF ORANGE COUNTY.

Sweet potatoes in all their varieties may properly be mentioned first as they seem to be indigenous to Florida. The "pioneer" raises them for the first crop on his newly cleared land and gets from fifty to three hundred bushels per acre, according to the quality of the land and the season. A single sprout once secured and he need never be without "seed." Every family has its potato patch or field.

Cow Peas, properly a field bean, flourish on almost any soil. There are many varieties, some yielding in six weeks after planting, and a continuous supply can be had from early spring to December. They are largely used both as snap and as shell beans and somewhat in the dry state. Fowls are very fond of them and the stems and leaves are eaten with avidity by cattle, both when green and when cured for hay. They yield a heavy crop.

Indian Corn is grown to some extent but less and less as orange culture increases, that and market gardening being so much more profitable. The yield on common pine land is ten to fifteen bushels per acre and double that on hammock.

but the yield might be largely increased by judicious fertilization.

Sugar Cane is cultivated quite extensively on both pine and hammock land, and is a profitable crop. Once set out it rattoons and yields for several years without replanting.

Long Staple Cotton does well in nearly every part of the county on both pine and hammock lands, and is of excellent quality and finds a ready cash market.

Rice grows readily, the soil being as favorable for its culture as any in Georgia or Carolina. It is an excellent and desirable crop.

Tobacco is well adapted to Orange county and can be cut several times the same season.

Arrowroot and Cassava yield abundant returns and make excellent food for the table, and also, for horses, cattle and other domestic animals. They are the greatest starch producers known. Hon. J. G. Sinclair has a mill for its manufacture near Orlando, and others will doubtless soon be erected in different parts of the county. The product is enormous.

Sisal Hemp, or Florida Jute, is indigenous to the soil and may be made a profitable industry.

The Pea Nut, or Pinder, thrives on ordinary land, requires but little cultivation and yields one hundred or more bushels per acre.

Chufas, another variety of ground nut, give large returns. They are chiefly grown for the fattening of swine, the animals doing their own harvesting.

Fibrous Plants generally can be produced with great success, both soil and climate appearing to be especially adapted to their luxuriant growth.

Oats, especially the rust proof varieties, give fair returns, but as yet are not largely cultivated.

Rye, Millet, etc., make excellent forage crops and will soon, no doubt, be cultivated quite extensively.

GRASSES.

The whole country is covered with native grasses: highlands and lowlands, pine, hammock, prairie and savanna. Most of them, however, are rather coarse and wiry when fully grown. Hence has been adopted the pernicious and destructive custom of burning over the lands every winter that the cattle might secure green and tender herbage. But the fire fiend is doomed and public sentiment and law will soon compel him to cease his ravages. He and the "pine rooter" will doubtless "vamoose" together.

The Bermuda grass is being introduced with great success, and all can have a grassy plat about their houses and green velvety walks. It also makes excellent feed for cattle and is much prized. The Johnson, or Guinea grass, also thrives well. Experiments now in progress will soon determine the best grasses to be cultivated in Orange county and a few years will unquestionably develop fine fields of forage.

MELONS, SQUASHES, ETC.

Soil and climate seem especially adapted to this class of products. They grow to large size and are of excellent quality.

GARDEN VEGETABLES.

The quantity and variety of all kinds of garden vegetables that thrive in both the Northern and Southern States is here only limited by the desire and ambition of the cultivator, and they can be plucked fresh every month in the year. Beans, peas, turnips, beets, carrots, parsnips, cabbage, cauliflower, celery, okra, egg plant, collards, Irish and sweet potatoes, melons, cucumbers, squashes, tomatoes and other vegetables too numerous to mention.

GARDENS.

The garden is planted at two special seasons, the early autumn and the early spring, but the whole range of vegetables is duplicated throughout the entire year, for a succession, though some plants do better at certain seasons than others. What to plant, when to plant, and how to cultivate and care for them must be learned by experience and observation of what the residents do to achieve success. The conditions are different from those in other states, and he who would be successful must intelligently adapt himself to circumstances. The experience of practical cultivators has not as yet been reduced to writing and compiled in a book, but the local newspapers are replete with many interesting experiences and in a few years some capable writer will doubtless publish a manual on Fruit and Vegetable Culture in the Orange Belt, the conditions here being materially different from those not only in other parts of the country but also in other parts of Florida. This central zone has conditions peculiar to itself, and he who desires success will heed them, learning by observation and experiment. The two prime conditions are an unstinted supply of fertilizer and of water. The intensive system of cultivation should be adopted. With that none need fail. At present less attention is given to gardens than at the North, the energies of the people being expended on their groves, but this condition is fast being remedied. Every family can and should have a magnificent garden with fresh fruit and vegetables every week in the year. Soil and climate afford the conditions necessary to success. Feed the soil and care for the plants and a bountiful crop is assured to a mathematical certainty.

SWINE.

Swine do well and every family can raise their own meat with very little trouble. Until recently the woods were full of them, but they are fast disappearing as the land is settled, the conditions proving unfavorable, but their place is better supplied with choice, home kept breeds.

SHEEP AND GOATS.

These animals do well here, but as yet, very little attention has been given them.

CATTLE.

All kinds of live stock thrive, good pasturage being afforded throughout the whole year. By attention to the growing of alternate forage crops every family can have milk and butter at all times, whether living near a natural range or otherwise.

HORSES AND MULES.

The native horses are very hardy animals, but the imported need a few months of easy work to become acclimated. Much of the teaming, plowing, etc., is done by mules.

POULTRY.

Orange county is par excellence the home of the poultry raiser. Chickens can be readily hatched and will thrive at all seasons of the year. Large quantities of eggs and fine fowls are easily produced in great abundance and at a comparatively trifling expense, while the demand is always very active and excellent prices are secured. Quick returns and handsome profits are assured.

GAME, FISH, ETC.

But a few short years ago and game was very abundant, but it is fast disappearing with the unprecedented rapid settlement of the county. Deer were plentiful as well as smaller game. Now deer and bear are found but occasionally near the settlements. Quail are quite plentiful, also ducks in the winter months. Cat and fox squirrels are quite numerous in some localities; coon, opossum and hares are also abundant. At rare intervals a wild cat or panther is the hunter's trophy.

Now and then the bark of a grey fox is heard and he is occasionally treed by the dogs. There are also a variety of birds; wild turkeys, heron of several varieties, and other water birds, some with beautiful plumage. In winter especially the fields and forests are alive with birds of kinds too numerous to mention, that furnish excellent sport for the huntsman.

The lakes and streams are well stocked with fish, hard and soft shelled turtle, etc., but their food supply is so abundant that they are not over anxious to be taken with the hook. The skillful fisherman, however, rarely goes unrewarded. Otter inhabit the streams and 'gators are seen occasionally but are rapidly diminishing in numbers.

REASONS FOR PREFERRING TO LOCATE IN ORANGE COUNTY.

1. It is below the line of destructive frosts.
2. It is the healthiest part of the healthful state of Florida.
3. It is more free from insect pests than any other part of the state, and as free as most parts of the Union.
4. The water in most parts of the county cannot be surpassed for purity and healthfulness and is better than in most localities.
5. It has a greater variety of soil and more choice and desirable locations than any other part of the State.
6. It preeminently abounds in beautiful lakes well stocked with fish, turtle, etc.
7. It is situated in the central portion of the peninsula, which is the narrowest part and the highest, thus giving it the purest and freshest breezes from both ocean and gulf, tempered and improved by filtration through the balsamic pine forests on either side.
8. It lies midway between the natural track of storms and tornadoes, and consequently is not subject to as frequent or severe storms as other parts of the country.
9. It is the natural physical center of the Orange Belt, and this luscious golden fruit here attains a perfection that is unequalled elsewhere, both tree and fruit.
10. Its climatic conditions and diversity of soil are such that a greater variety of fruits and vegetables can be grown in Orange county than in any other section of the country, if not of the globe.
11. Without derogation of other localities, it may truthfully be asserted that Orange county has a more wide awake, enterprising, moral, highly cultured, well-to-do population than any other county.
12. It is increasing faster in population, wealth, new

villages, cultivated fields, populous centers, enterprising merchants, etc., and in fact in all the elements and privileges that constitute modern civilization than any other section.

13. Nowhere can one secure a competence in so short a time, with the endurance of so few hardships, and with so little deprivation of the privileges to which he or she has been accustomed as in Orange county.

14. Its climate is the most delicious and healthful that the known world affords. The days are pleasant, charming, delightful, and the nights are cool, tranquil, and refreshing. The temperature is not subject to sudden changes, yet there is sufficient variety to keep the physical and mental powers healthfully attuned to energetic action, and prevent that feeling of languor and lassitude so common where the thermometric changes are less and unvarying, as in some tropical islands.

WHO SHOULD NOT COME TO ORANGE COUNTY.

1. Neither those who are *perfectly* contented where they are, nor those who are always dissatisfied.

2. Neither lazy people, dishonest people, nor grumblers nor growlers are wanted. The country is fast settling up with a very different class and they would not acclimatize readily.

3. Those who cannot leave old acquaintances and old associations, form new and adapt themselves to changed conditions should stay where they are. At any rate they should not come to Orange county.

4. Those who do not like warm weather, and to whom chilly winds, frost, ice and snow are a special delight, should stay away. Such luxuries Orange county does not afford.

5. Those who must live among rocks and hills, turbulent streams, and icy mountains should seek some other locality.

6. Those who expect to secure fortunes without labor; those who are content only in large cities, and those who are unwilling to endure some present discomfort to realize their ambitions for the future, should stay away. Orange county is no place for such.

7. Those who desire to engage in general farming as practiced at the North and West should stay there. This is a fruit and vegetable country.

8. Those who cannot be content unless doing heavy work and toiling from daylight to dark in mud or slush, or in snow or ice, should not come to Orange county for the conditions here are the opposite. The regular work is mostly

light and requires the exercise of brain quite as much, if not more, than muscle.

WHO SHOULD COME TO ORANGE COUNTY.

1. Those who can adapt themselves to changed conditions, can make new acquaintances and form new associations to take the place of the old and will strive to do their best whatever the circumstances in which they are placed.

2. Those who prefer a mild climate, pure air, bright sunny days and pleasant weather generally, instead of chilly winds and storms of sleet and snow.

3. Those who desire to better their condition; those willing to labor and to wait; those who prefer to secure a large income from a small piece of ground, rather than to cultivate many acres for a small income.

4. In brief, those who have eyes with which they see, ears with which they hear, and understandings that enable them to perceive and improve some of the many opportunities and advantages that are afforded here, such cannot fail to do well by coming to Orange county, as thousands of others have done and are doing.

5. To all predisposed to or suffering from pulmonary consumption, asthma, bronchitis, catarrh, hay fever, inflammatory rheumatism, malaria, and like diseases, Orange county offers a city of refuge and restoration.

6. Those who desire their children to escape many of the ills incident to childhood, and to grow up strong and healthful will find that Orange county offers many advantages. Diphtheria, croup, cholera infantum, scarlet fever and malignant fevers generally, as well as several other diseases are unknown here.

PROGRESS OF ORANGE COUNTY.

The rapidity and the substantial character of the settlement and the development of this favored county is truly marvelous, and its advancement is progressing in a geometrical ratio. With a population of 73 in 1840, of 466 in 1850, of 987 in 1860, and in 1870 of only 2,195, with no manufactories, nor hardly a store worthy the name, with virtually no orange groves, with no newspapers, no schools, no churches, and unknown to the world, it is now the most enterprising and rapidly developing section of the State, and probably is not excelled, if equalled, by any locality in America, and it bids fair to be the most wealthy and prosperous as well as the most healthful area on the globe.

The population in 1880 had increased to 6,190, and is now estimated to be at least 15,000, with strong reasons for expecting it will gain several thousands the present season. The taxable property in 1871, as shown by the assessor's books, was $480,611. In 1880 it had increased to $1,394,-141; in 1881 to $1,711,174; in 1882 to $2,338,764, and in 1883 to $3,379,824, the increase in three years being $1,985,683, and it has gained many thousands since the assessment, the increase being nearly two millions in three years. It now has seven handsome and ably edited newspapers with a possibility of several more the coming season. The public schools now number eighty-nine and quickened attention is being given to education. Churches have been built in all the more prominent localities and regular services are held by all the leading denominations, the school houses being used in the less developed localities. Stores have multiplied and increased all over the county, and they are well stocked with choice assortments of goods. Prices are very reasonable. Postoffices too, forty-two in number, are conveniently located and frequent mails keep the people in close communication with other parts of the world. There are also several well managed railroad lines and others are being rapidly constructed. Also, several lines of telegraph, and the telephone is not a stranger. The hum of the saw is heard and numerous steam mills are running day and night, unable to keep pace with the demand for lumber, for new houses and other buildings are springing up as if by magic all over the county. Roads have been laid out in every direction, good substantial bridges have been built, and everything betokens an active era of increasing prosperity. New clearings are almost numberless, and orange, lemon, lime and guava groves and pine apple orchards may be counted by thousands. Manufactories of various kinds are also being erected. Excellent hotels are numerous, also private boarding houses, and on every hand are unmistakable evidences of prosperity.

FINANCIAL STATUS.

By reference to the books of the County Recorder we find that the real estate transactions from January 1st to July 1st, 1883, aggregate $984,240, which gives a slight idea of the activity of real estate. A large part has been purchased by people from other sections who are making homes in Orange county. Those who sell do not leave the county but reinvest in other lands, or devote the amounts received to the improvement of their remaining acres. This in part accounts for the increase of over one million dollars of taxable property the past year. New clearings, new houses, and new groves are to be seen in all parts of the county.

The following figures will give a fair idea of the prosperous and healthful financial condition of this section. It is taken from the County Auditor's report to the Grand Jury at the last term of Court, and we are assured substantially expresses the present condition of the treasury. It must also be borne in mind that not only is the county free of debt, with this surplus in the treasury for the present year's expenses, but that it also has the county tax of $56,444 in addition, that will be collected during the next three months, to be applied to regular expenses and to the development of the county.

Too much praise cannot be accorded our able and efficient Board of County Commissioners for their wise and far-sighted action in keeping the County's affairs abreast of the needs of the times, and they have very sensibly builded wisely for the future while giving proper attention to present needs. Their aim has been to develop the County, and its present wonderful prosperity shows how well they have done their work. The rate of taxation has averaged about fifteen mills, and is sixteen this year on a low valuation, but the new roads, the substantial bridges, the improvements on public buildings, the liberal and fostering care of public schools, etc., show that the money has been well and judiciously expended.

The financial record reads as follows:

GENERAL REVENUE ACCOUNT.

Due the Fund by the Treasurer,		$ 749.49
" " " Collector,		2,442.35
" " " State		50.63
Total due the Fund		$3,242.47
Warrants Outstanding,		2,043.95
Balance unexpended,		$1,198.52

COUNTY BUILDING FUND.

Due the Fund by the Treasurer,		$2,409.75
" " " Collector		1,264.66
" " " State,		50.82
Total due the Fund,		$3,725.23
Warrants outstanding,		546.36
Balance unexpended,		$3,178.87

SCHOOL FUND ACCOUNT.

Due by Treasurer,	- - - - -	$1,697.00
" Collector,	- - - - - -	1,946.66
" State	- - - - - -	76.27
Total due the Fund,	- - - -	$3,719.93
Warrants outstanding,	- - - -	501.94
Balance unexpended,	- - - -	$3,217.99

There is also due the several Funds by the State, $1,536.02
T. J. SHINE, Auditor.

The County is entirely out of debt, the policy being to "pay as you go." By summing up the unexpended balances we find the sum of $7,595.38 on hand to meet current expenses, until the assessment of $56,444 taxes is collected.

In 1883, there will be expended on roads $3,380; for schools $13,519, in addition to the $3,380 received from the State revenue from the one mill tax, and the numerous private subscriptions, which amount is annually increasing.

GENERAL TEMPERATURE.

Many people have ignorantly had the idea that though the climate during the winter months is delightful it must be oppressively hot in summer; but this is a mistake. Many of the residents consider the summers even more enjoyable than the winters, and our own experience convinces us that the summer months are more agreeable here than in any other part of the Union. It is also the season when work is not pressing and opportunities are afforded for agreeable leisure. The air is rarely, or never, sultry, and the only requirement for a cool, enjoyable place is to get in the shade. Every day furnishes a quantum of cool, delicious breezes from Ocean or Gulf. The air, too, is less humid most of the year than in the famous dry climate of Minnesota. The thermometer never indicates as high a temperature in summer nor as low in winter as in any of the other states, and persons can live out of doors comfortably the year around. In fact, some now wealthy were too poor when they first came here to build houses, and lived in tents. Yet a good house, though not as necessary, is as enjoyable here as elsewhere. It should have broad halls and wide piazzas festooned with the flowering vines and beautiful plants that here grow luxuriantly the year round. Every one can easily have an abode of beauty if taste and inclination so dictate.

Tables of thermometric temperature might be given, but no just idea of the heat that is *felt* can be gained from them, the pure fresh air counteracting the depressing effects of high temperature that, oppressive elsewhere, is delicious and enjoyable here.

To satisfy the incredulous, we give a summary of the weather for the summer of 1883, the hottest summer for years, as shown by the records of the U. S. Signal Office, at Sanford, Florida. As regards the winters, every one knows that they are the most delicious possible, and especially favorable for invalids.

AVERAGE TEMPERATURE.

1883.— June, 80.5   July, 83.5   August, 80.9.
For the three summer months, 81.6

MAX. TEM.	MIN. TEM.
June..................98.0	June..................71.0
July..................99.4	July..................70.0
August..................96.9	August..................69.0

MEAN RELATIVE HUMIDITY.

June, 78.7..........   July, 72.7..........   August, 77.1..........
Point of total saturation 100.

TOTAL RAINFALL.

June, 8.57 inches..........   July, 3.14 inches..........   August, 6.74 inches..........

PREVAILING DIRECTION OF WIND.

June, Southwest..........   July, Southwest..........   August, Southeast..........

A FEW FACTS AND REFLECTIONS.

Though the highest average summer temperature is only 83 degrees and the very highest any day of summer but 99.4 degrees, quite a number of degrees less than at the North and West and other parts of the country, yet the winter temperature is even more favorable and congenial, very rarely going below 40 degrees. Once, and once only last winter was it as low as 33 degrees, or below 40 degrees at our residence, and very thin ice formed in some places. But none of the citrus fruits or even the tender guavas were injured in the least, though it somewhat damaged the pine apples in exposed localities where unprotected. The sensitive pepper trees, however, endured the three or four light frosts without harm and bear bountifully the present year. So generous is Orange county's lake protection that the few occasional light frosts, that occur some years, are less destructive here than in localities many miles to the southward. The physical conformation of the country is, also, very advantageous in this respect. The absence of mud and dust should also be especially noted. It is a surprise to all.

Men—white men—can and do work at all hours of the day, and every secular day in the year, at their ordinary avocations, and that, too, with less discomfort than in any other part of the Union. One can accomplish much more here than elsewhere, for he has more favorable days and hours for work and does not have to overtax his system by severe labor during the hottest months, the busiest time being in the cooler season. The nights, too, are so pleasantly cool and delicious that everyone is able to secure sweet and refreshing sleep every night and thus fortify the system for the trials and duties of each succeeding day. The mornings the most of the year are like those delicious June mornings at the North, when all nature seems atune and instinct with joyous life. Mornings such as one remembers even in his dreams. No hot, sultry, stifling nights when one pants and gasps for a breath of fresh air, but pure, cool, healthful and delicious mornings. The midday heats of summer are intense when exposed to the direct rays of the sun and perspiration flows profusely, but get in a shade, either natural or artificial, and a delicious sense of coolness is felt at once. But nature provides this shade at oft recurring intervals, and such a thing as an entirely cloudless day is almost unknown.

As Old Sol pours down his almost tropical heat in the mid hours of the mid-summer days, evaporation from Ocean and Gulf and the many lakes and rivers is very active, and the heavens are soon overcast with clouds that flitting hither and thither interpose a quenching shield to Appollo's fiery darts, and the genial breezes from old Ocean's broad expanse bear away the excessive caloric. Then, too, oft on summer afternoons the powers of the air engage in strife, the forked lightnings play, the thunders roll, and a delicious rainfall cools the super-heated atmosphere and refreshes all vegetable as well as animal life. The rain comes at the season when most needed and vegetation thrives at a wonderful pace. No clouds of dust are seen enveloping the weary traveler and making life a burden, as in most other parts of the Union.

Orange county is a white man's country and there are fewer negroes here than in other parts of the South. The white man here can do his own work, whatever it may be, without the aid of the 14th Amendment, or any other assistance except the amendment engrafted in his own constitution by right habits and the delicious climate of Orange county. It has nowhere a peer, and as its wonderful virtues become more widely and more thoroughly known, those desiring to enjoy life in its best conditions, and those suffering from the fell power of disease, will here find the fountains of joyous health and superabundant life in its best and choicest conditions, in both winter and summer. Its people will be the most wealthy, independent, happy, intelligent and cultivated of any on the face of the habitable globe. Its whole area will be a perfect garden thickly dotted with happy homes, embowered amid delicious groves of the choicest fruits and beautified by superabundant flowers that bloom all the year.

THE DEATH RATE.

The death rate in Florida as compared with Italy is as 3 to 5, the rate per thousand being 11.72 in Florida to 19.98 in Italy. But this estimate includes the whole State, whereas in Orange county alone the death rate is but 5.4, and in that wonderfully low rate are included numbers of invalids who come here too enfeebled for their systems to respond to the enequalled curative effects of the delightful climate. This is the most healthful section of a very healthy State.

As regards malarial diseases the number of cases of deaths, as shown by the records of the United States army, is in Florida but one to 287 cases, while in the Southern Military Division it is one to 54, in the Northern one to 52, and in the Middle one to 36. Yet Orange county is twice as healthful as the State at large.

EDUCATIONAL FACILITIES AND PROGRESS.

Though Orange county is young in years it is not behind other localities in educational interests and progress in improved educational facilities.

The first Board of Education in this county was organized December 11, 1869, and the second meeting was held May 27, 1871, when there were six public schools with 150 pupils. In 1875 the schools had increased to seventeen; in 1877 to twenty-six, in 1879 to forty-two, and in 1880 to fifty-two, with 3,264 pupils; in 1882 to seventy-eight, with 3,718 pupils. During the present year, 1883, additional schools have been established, making the present number eighty-nine, six of which are for colored pupils. More schools will doubtless be established the present season, the laws of Florida and the feeling of the Board of Education being very favorable toward supplying all needs. As is seen by the great progress of the past twelve years, their aim is to keep the educational interests well abreast of the country's material development, and the next decade will undoubtedly witness a development in an accelerating ratio. Higher grades of schools will be established and increased qualifications be demanded of teachers. In fact, the citizens generally are becoming alive to the importance of a better education for their children, for rapid progress and advancement is the motto of Orange county.

In Orlando, a non-sectarian University under the auspices of the M. E. Church, is opened in a beautiful building with a full corps of teachers selected from various denominations, and it is proposed to make it an educational institution of the highest order, preparing such pupils as may desire for a college course. It will also afford instruction in music and in art.

COST OF AN ORANGE GROVE.

First is the cost of the land, which depends on the location and the views of the owner. Of course the nearer a populous center the higher the price, but it will be from $1.25 an acre (very scarce) to 100 times that amount: average from $15 to $50. The south, or southeast side of a lake is very decidedly preferable. Clearing of trees and grubbing out roots costs from $12 to $30 per acre. Plowing $3: cost of trees and setting from 25 cents to $1 each. Trees bring double what they did two years ago, so great is the demand. Care of a grove and fertilizer is from $25 to $50 per acre. The higher price with the better man in charge is the best investment. About fifty trees should be set to the acre, for permanency, but a better show, temporarily, is obtained by setting one-half the distance apart, but we do not advise it. As a general rule each tree should have one dollar's worth of fertilizer and labor applied to it each year until it comes into bearing, say six years. After that one-fourth to one-fifth of the proceeds of the grove should be applied to it to keep it in vigorous condition. These are only general average estimates and may be varied by especial conditions. However, the growing of a productive grove of the citrus family is as much a matter of mathematical certainty as the raising of a herd of cattle or a drove of hogs. The first requirement is good stock and proper quarters; the second intelligent care and a sufficient amount of appropriate food. Plants as well as animals must be properly fed and cared for. After six years the grove properly fertilized and cared for, will more than repay the expense, and after ten years will yield a handsome income. Some of the trees will yield five hundred, some a thousand, and some two thousand or more. Call the average 1,000 per tree and the yield is 50,000 per acre. This at the average price on the tree, $15.00 per M, is $750 per acre, and as the trees grow older the amount will annually increase. In orange growing there is very much less danger of loss from disease and unpropitious climatic conditions than in the raising of live stock. The average price is also more sure and less liable to fluctuation. The growing of a grove is, also, the most pleasant possible of occupations, both physical and mental powers being called into pleasant and healthful activity. Other crops can also be grown on the same ground the first few years. In short, an outlay of a dollar a year for from six to ten years, gives a tree that will yield an income of ten to thirty dollars per year and steadily increasing.

RELIGIOUS INTERESTS.

All denominations, especially the Baptists, Methodists, Presbyterians and Episcopalians, are very active and church and Sunday school services are held in all parts of the county. All the important centers have church buildings, others are building, and the school houses are utilized in other localities. No fear but Orange county will be a land of churches, literary and other societies, as well as the locality for lovely and happy homes.

POLITICS.

This is a great "bug-bear" with many who do not understand the situation. Virtually there is no politics here as supposed at the north. The people are too busy in their race to be millionaires to devote their time to politics, and one rarely hears it mentioned in conversation. By force of habit about election time the papers have a series of articles more or less virulent and some of the local orators endeavor to enthuse. Election day comes and passes off quietly, but many of the citizens take too little interest in the matter to go to the polls and the democrats score a few hundred majority, though there are undoubtedly nearly as many republicans as democrats in the county. Our experience here satisfies us that there is even less coercion and intimidation here than in most other parts of the country. The question here is not "what is a man's politics?" but, how large a grove has he, and how is it progressing?

ST. JOHNS & LAKE EUSTIS RAILWAY.

The only line touching Lakes Eustis, Dora, Harris, Yale, Griffin and soon to reach Apopka, which makes it the GREAT LAKE REGION LINE of Florida, connecting daily with all steamers of the People's Line and De Bary-Baya Merchant's Line on the St. Johns River, via ASTOR, to and from

BRYANVILLE,	SUMMIT,	RAVENSWOOD,
ALTOONA,	GLENDALE,	UMATILLA,
FORT MASON,	EUSTIS,	MOUNT HOMER,
TAVARES,	LANE PARK,	

thence by Lake Steamer to ASTATULA, YALAHA, BLOOMFIELD, HELENA, COOLEY ISLAND, and LEESBURG.

Branch road to Orange Bend, and will soon be extended to Leesburg.

Accommodations complete. Hotels at Astor, Ravenswood, Altoona, Fort Mason, Eustis, Tavares, Astatula, Yalaha and Leesburg. From Summit to Fort Mason the lands are high and rolling, with clear water lakes thickly scattered along the line of road, which for beauty cannot be surpassed by any of their kind in the State.

For particulars relative to railroad lands, or other information, apply at the General Office at Fort Mason.

W. J. JARVIS,
    Superintendent.

W. H. TREADWELL,
    G. F. & P. Agt.

ACRON.

This settlement occupies a pleasant tract of rolling, high pine land in township 22 south, ranges 27 and 28 east, and contains about 60,000 acres, almost surrounded by beautiful lakes and streams of running water. Alexander Spring river on the northern boundary being large enough for navigation. It has its source in a fine spring about 75 yards across and 35 feet deep, the height of the water varying but little in either wet or dry seasons. The stream enters the St. John's about two miles above Bluffton. The settlement is nine and one-half miles due west of Hawkinsville and five east of the St. Johns, (Astor) & Lake Eustis railroad. It is on the line of the proposed Jacksonville, Tampa & Key West railroad.

Acron dates from the autumn of 1876, when J. H. Campbell, Esq., one of our present efficient board of county commissioners, and a few friends from Rock Island county, Ill., settled there and commenced improvements. It now has fifty-five families and single men living on their places, and 61 groves owned by non residents. Each grove will average 500 trees, 40 per cent of which are fruiting. It has a postoffice and a tri-weekly mail, a good school building and public school with about 35 pupils; preaching two Sundays in the month by a Methodist preacher and once by a Presbyterian. The society is sociable, peaceable and law-abiding. They have a steam saw mill with first-class machinery for dressing lumber. Rough lumber sells for $12 per M. The water is sweet, clear and pure and obtained at a depth of 10 to 65 feet. There is probably no more healthful location in the world, persons who with their families have lived there the past eight years never having had occasion for the services of a physician. The land is considered first-class pine and can be bought at $10 to $15 per acre. A country store with a capital of $1,500 to $2,000 would do well there.

Oranges, lemons, limes, guavas, Japan plums and persimmons, pine apples, figs, Le Conte pears, grapes, strawberries, mulberries, wild plums, peaches, etc., are successfully raised there, and corn, sugar cane, oats, rye, Irish and sweet potatoes, and all kinds of garden truck and vegetables are grown for home use.

For further particulars address the postmaster at Acron, who, though not a land agent, yet feels an interest in the development of this fair country in general and his own locality in particular.

ALTOONA AND VICINITY.

Altoona is located on the St. Johns & Lake Eustis Railroad, 18 miles from Astor on the St. Johns, and 8 miles from Lake Eustis. The town is built upon rolling land but recently covered with a heavy growth of pine. It is 110 feet above the St. Johns river and 60 feet above Lake Eustis. The streets are laid off parallel with the rail road on both sides, and the corporate limits are washed by the waters of Lakes Minneola, King, Pearl, Daisy, Ouida, and Linn, all beautiful clear water lakes well stocked with fish.

Two years ago there was not more than half a dozen families in this neighborhood, and a pine forest grew where now stands a thriving little town, which contains three general stores, one drug store, one jewelry shop, one wagon and blacksmith shop, one saw and planing mill, one hotel and several boarding houses, one church, one livery stable, and one weekly paper, "The Altoona Argus." Neat and tasteful residences are being built, the streets and fronts cleared up, and in many ways the cross roads settlement is beginning to assume city airs.

There is but one bearing grove in sight. This was planted by Mr. F. J. Hinson, and was sold by him about July 10th to Mr. Rumph, of Arkansas, for ten thousand dollars. It covers ten acres, is first-class pine land, and can boast of one hundred trees under four years old now loaded with fruit.

Experience has demonstrated that the best of our pine lands are, for many reasons, the most satisfactory orange lands, being easy to clear and cultivate, but any who prefer the richer hammock land can also be accommodated, as the hammocks of Nigger Town Creek are only from two to three miles distant, where bodies of rich land can be yet bought. In view of the fact that older settlements in the county have become better known, and more thickly settled, more widely advertised, we do not say, "come and see the *best* corner of Orange," but we do say, "see it all before you purchase." Here you will find an industrious, energetic people and most of them "here for good,"—not winter visitors—you will find our lands first-rate and prices reasonable. Our section has wrought many wonderful cures in consumptive cases, and many of our citizens have located here on account of such troubles, and in every instance have found relief.

Come and see us!

UMATILLA.

On the St. Johns & Lake Eustis R. R., twenty miles from Astor is Umatilla Station. For miles in every direction, but particularly east and west, are fertile lands capable of producing corn, cotton and sugar cane, as well as sweet potatoes, cassava and arrow root and as suitable for the production of tropical fruit as any in South Florida, dotted and adorned with lakes, offering building sites of unsurpassed beauty. We invite investigation and challenge comparison with the most advertised locality in this section of our State. Until within two years our people have been self-supporting, relying almost wholly upon farming, and large quantities of Sea Island cotton have been marketed at this point. Now land is being cleared and planted with orange trees, those now bearing giving satisfactory evidence of the certainty of success and we invite you to visit the famous McEwen grove and see for yourself how industry will supply the lack of capital and bring abundant reward. Within a few steps of the depot is the thriving grove of Mr. Trowell. It will reward you to visit it. The first settlement was made here twenty-two years ago. The population in two years has trebled and this has been purely because of our solid advantages in health, soil and production. We have not employed agents or advertised. Vegetables have been largely grown with abundant profit. Orange, lemon and lime trees are healthy and vigorous, and the tender guava is now loaded with fruit.

A good school with nearly 100 pupils, a Baptist church with 100 members, and Methodist and Presbyterian churches within easy distance are evidences of the peaceable, law abiding, moral status of our community. One store and another building afford all needed supply. A saw mill at the station is now offering lumber at $10 per M. We also have a grist mill, and thus are ready to provide shelter and bread.

Within a radius of three miles there are large quantities of hammock land for those who desire to embark in either fruit or vegetable growing, near depot and with quick transportation. These lands can be bought cheaply as compared with their value.

This locality is noted for health, with lakes once seen, a thing of beauty, a joy forever. Lands are cheaper in price than in any other favorite locality. We invite investigation and settlement. We desire the advantages that larger populations have over sparsely settled communities, and we desire that you shall have and enjoy, as we do, the more than comfort of this delightful region.

FORT MASON.

Fort Mason, situated on Lake Eustis, has been for three years the terminus of the St. Johns & Lake Eustis Railroad. It has two large general stores, kept by Chas. T. Smith & Co. and S. M. Owens & Co., and a large, new, well kept hotel. There is a large scope of good, cultivatable land within a short distance of this town, which is well suited to vegetable as well as orange growing, owing to the water protection of Lakes Eustis and Yale. The lands adjacent are better adapted than many places farther south. One of the greatest advantages this part of Orange county enjoys is its facilities for transporting freight. This winter and next spring fruit and vegetable growers will not only be able to ship their produce via the St. Johns & Lake Eustis Road to the St. Johns river, but will have connection with the North via the Florida Southern R. R. It would be well for persons who contemplate settling in Florida to examine in person, or by letter, this particular section of the State. There are advantages to be secured by settlers here which are not found in any other locality. There is a large body of unimproved land which can be bought at fair prices and on good terms, which will quickly enhance in value. Instances can be given to show that early vegetables are being grown very profitably on Lakes Yale and Eustis, while the young orange groves are coming on.

Fort Mason is in what is known as "The Lake Region" of South Florida, lying on Lake Eustis, which is a large and beautiful body of water, connected by steam boats with Lakes Harris, Griffin, Dora, Beauclair and Apopka, and having direct communication with the towns of Leesburg, Yalaha, Esperance, Helena, on Lake Harris, and Eustis and Tavares, both by rail and water. There is a tract of about 2,000 acres, lying between Lakes Eustis and Yale, of high pine land through which the Orange Bend Branch of the St. Johns & Lake Eustis road runs, which could be bought in lots to suit purchasers of from ten acres upwards, which would make pretty and profitable homes for any persons wanting to engage in fruit and vegetable growing. This section of the country is as healthful as any in the State.

SENECA.

This is a fast growing little town on the lake of the same name, situated five miles east from Eustis and about the same distance from Ft. Mason, Mt. Dora and Sorrento. The section of country around Seneca is noted for its beauty and healthfulness, its entire freedom from malarial fever, and the fertility of the soil. The lands are high and rolling, no swamps, but many beautiful clear water lakes. For the growth of oranges and other citrus fruits, pine apples, etc., they are unsurpassed by any lands in the State. Most of our oldest citizens settled here after a careful canvass of all the southern counties, and the result of a few years cultivation of their groves has proven the wisdom of their choice.

We have instances right here, proving that a man with small capital can start a five acre grove, and with judicious cultivation and the use of but little fertilizer, have it advance in value at the rate of $1,000 per annum until in full bearing. Mr. R. F. Finley came here seven years ago with but little means and no experience or knowledge of the business. He cleared his land, set out his trees, has cultivated them entirely with his own hands, and to-day his grove is cheap for $10,000. Mr. Bramhall, Mr. Cooper, Mrs. Drawdy, Mr. Kelly, and many others furnish like instances. Mr. Ely Cooper is our oldest settler. He came here twenty-five years ago, and settled near the east end of the lake. He has reared and supported a large family—ten children—by ordinary farming, without even the aid of what was so common, the keeping of cattle. He did not turn his attention to orange growing as a business until about seven years ago, but had planted a few trees for his own use only. Some of these trees, now thirteen years old, have 2,000 oranges each.

The large grove of 130 acres owned by the S. E. Orange Grove Co., of Washington, D. C., is located here. The land was selected by Cols. J. A. Macdonald and M. J. Taylor, gentlemen long resident in Florida and good judges of land. This fact alone is proof of the superior quality of our land if other evidence was needed.

We have a large and constantly increasing area in grove, but have plenty of land for all new comers. Some large tracts have but lately been placed upon the market, and are now offered cheap to actual settlers in lots to suit. Our country is rapidly filling up, and lands double in value every year. Our town is growing rapidly, and, occupying as it does, the exact center of West Orange, on the line of two projected railroads, one of which, the Jacksonville, Tampa,

& Key West, is now building. It will undoubtedly be chosen as the site of a new county if one should be set off soon, as talked of.

Our people are mostly from the Northern and Western States, and extend a cordial welcome to the new comer and every facility needed to make himself a home can be had here. Our large, new saw mill is turning out the best lumber at $13 per M. Our stores furnish groceries, hardware, stoves, furniture, etc., and we have every school and church privilege that can be desired. Our academy is large and well furnished and schools well attended. We have preaching three Sundays each month. Sabbath school every Sunday and choir practice, with organ accompaniment, every Saturday evening.

Besides this we have a society called the "Lightfoot Club." It is composed of our best citizens, and is in the interest of public improvement, immigration, etc. It proposes to furnish reliable information to all people about to immigrate, and guard them from imposition and swindles.

Parties wishing to know more of Seneca, with a view of becoming settlers, could not do better than to address the corresponding secretary of this club.

M. H. WADSWORTH,
Seneca, via Ft. Mason.

THE SORRENTO REGION.

What is known as the Sorrento Region lies in the western part of Orange county and embraces the high, rolling pine lands between the Wekiva river and the large lakes which form the headwaters of the Ocklawaha. Its elevation is from 100 to 200 feet above the St. Johns river, and its surface is rolling and undulating and presents a most pleasing and varied appearance. It is covered with a heavy growth of tall pines, free from underbrush and producing a heavy growth of the various grasses indigenous to Florida. A number of small lakes situated among the hills tend to enhance the beauty of the landscapes. Its elevation, and the undulating conformation of its surface, prevents its being flooded during wet seasons as many other parts are, and being free from swamps it is one of the most healthy spots in Florida, fevers, the curse of the low lands, being almost entirely unknown here. The settlement of Sorrento commenced in the winter of 1875 and 1876, and since that time its progress has been steady and permanent, the settlers being of an industrious, substantial class, principally from the Northern states.

The last two years the increase in population has been very rapid and the prospects are good for a still more rapid increase during the coming year.

The exact number of the inhabitants of this region is not known, but we can count 220 land owners within the delivery of the Sorrento postoffice. The village of Sorrento has two stores, a hotel and a building devoted to church and school purposes; also a postoffice and telegraph office. A Methodist Episcopal church has been organized here, Rev. Mr. Edwards officiating. Services are also held once a month by Rev. Mr. Enloe of the Presbyterian denomination; also occasional services by Rev. W. C. Brooks, Universalist, and others. A Union Sabbath school is in a flourishing condition, and a public day school commenced the first of September. Two saw mills furnish us with plenty of lumber both dressed and rough, flooring, shingles, etc., in fact everything needed in building.

The principal business of this community is raising orange groves, for which this region seems specially adapted. The lemon and lime also flourish here and receive a good share of attention. The number of trees in grove is very large, but the settlement being only seven years old, only a few groves are yet in bearing. The pine apple succeeds admirably and thousands of plants are being set out the present season. Nearly all other semi-tropical fruits do well here, but our space is too small to mention them in detail. The Wekiva river on the east and the Ocklawaha and the St. Johns & Lake Eustis Railroad on the west are our present means of transportation, but the prospects ahead are for two more railroads to intersect each other somewhere near Sorrento. Persons desiring further information regarding this prosperous and rapidly growing community, can obtain such information by enclosing five cents in stamps to the postmaster at Sorrento, Florida, for a large map and descriptive circular of this region in which is marked the groves, lakes, roads, buildings and the names of the persons owning the lands. Also a list of the different kinds of business carried on, the names of the public officers, etc.

MOUNT DORA.

One year ago this place was an unbroken forest with scarcely a tree cut. The natural attractions and advantages of the spot had, however, been known for some time by two or three long headed, wide awake gentlemen, who carefully watched as transportation facilities approached, and when the right time arrived drove their stakes, christened the new born town and published to the world that it lived, into it had been breathed the breath of life and it moved and had a being. And here, nestling so quietly and so beautifully by Lake Dora's side, overlooking lake and vale, and in the far distance, twenty miles away, the mountain tops in Sumpter county, on Lake Apopka's western shores, are plainly visible; here, 300 feet above the level of the sea, and but 50 miles away; here with the grand old hills all about you; here with the fresh breezes from ocean and gulf, tempered and softened by the journey through the pine forests; here gradually sloping back from the water is our beautiful town and the future great sanitarium of Orange county—Mount Dora. Twelve months rolled by and what do we see—our present prosperous, healthy, inviting town. As a health resort we affirm it is second to none in the State, nay, more than this, we challenge comparison from any standpoint that can be chosen. The beach of the lake is a white sand, firm as a drive or a walk; here and there the beautiful cabbage palmetto sends its semi-tropical head towering above its neighbors, which lends a charm to the scene as you look over the lake and the lakes beyond, which are partly hidden from view by charming islands of palm. This landscape is at once a park, regal and tropical to the new comer. The high rolling pine lands with which the town is surrounded are unexcelled for the production of the orange, lemon, lime, pineapple and guava, in fact all semi-tropical fruits, as can be seen by the many groves old and young. There are also heavier lands which can be had at reasonable figures and terms for the production of all kinds of vegetables. All the lands here, whether town or rural property, compare favorably in price with locations that cannot compare with this. The exceptionally moral and pleasant character of the settlers, with the efforts being made to influence that class of settlers yet to come, its easy access of communication, all this, added to an atmosphere of purity, free from miasmatic influences, and with hotel accommodations already surpassing that of any town in west Orange, where the care, comfort and welfare of their guests is the first consideration, and all necessary medical aid can be had first-class and efficient, we are surely warranted in saying to the invalid, the overtaxed business man, the sportsman, or pleasure seeker, this place cannot be equalled. To the permanent settler in Florida, where can you do better? Health is the first consideration. If you cannot find and keep it here, it is useless to look in any place for it. Come and see, we do not exaggerate. The half has not been told, and for beauty, picturesqueness and attractiveness our truly beautiful town cannot be excelled. We have three large hotels, a credit to any place, twenty-four dwelling houses, eight more building and contracted for, a wagon and blacksmith shop, carpenter shop, boat builder, a large general store, and a drug store soon to be erected. Mount Dora is situated in west Orange county, latitude 28½ degrees. Take the steamer from Jacksonville to Astor, thence by railroad to Tavares, and by boat across Lake Dora, and you are landed at the future great winter resort of the State of Florida.

TANGERINE.

Of this beautiful locality, Hon. D. W. Adams, who had spent two winters in our State looking for a suitable locality in which to settle, recently wrote:

"One January evening, I came unto the hills overlooking Lake Beauclaire just as the sun was going down in a blaze of glory. The air was as soft as the breath of peace. The pines, the palms, the gorgeous coloring of the clouds and sky and setting sun were repeated in mirrored waters. To the north, Lake Dora half encircled beautiful Beauclaire in her crimson embrace, while to the south Ola and Carleton (Sams) glistened through the pines like gems of purest water, in emerald settings. Back from the lake for miles sweep the grand swelling hills and lovely secluded valleys, all adorned by those long leaved pines, tall, slender and graceful, the sure indication of a soil peculiarly adapted to the growth of the famous Florida orange. Here and there, less in size but no less beautiful, Lakes Angeline, Fanny, Lilly, Gem, Victoria, Bonnet, Terry, Lena, etc., add beauty to the landscape, and anon a spring of sparkling water delights and entices the thirsty traveler.

Here and there commanding hills in these beautiful valleys by these sparkling waters, among these health-giving pines, surrounded by lovely lakes to furnish sport to the angler, food to the hungry, and to bear our freights and pleasure yachts; here is Tangerine, our home, the gem of Florida. From this point the waters flow north by the Ocklawaha river, east to the St. Johns, west to the gulf. Located as we are on this high rolling plateau, the summit of the peninsula, midway between the ocean and gulf, we are constantly refreshed and our climate equalized by the ever recurring sea and gulf breezes, and are comparatively exempt from the gales that sweep the coasts. The summer days are cooled, and by the same agency the frost is taken from the winter winds. Just northwest of us, a cluster of five large lakes, Harris, Griffin, Eustis, Dora and Beauclaire, furnishes an additional equalizer, giving us a location eminently adapted to the culture of very tender plants and trees. Even the great freezing cold wave of December 30, 1880, spent its fury on their northern shores; and here the lime and lemon, tenderest of all the citrus family, were uninjured in leaf, twig and blossom.

This is no diminutive "town site," owned by speculators and held at fancy prices, but a broad expanse of the finest orange land in Florida; miles in extent, sufficient for a large and powerful settlement, owned and occupied by actual settlers. We have made roads, planted 15,000 orange and lemon trees, established mail routes, saw mills, a postoffice with daily mail, store, schools, Sunday school and religious services. We have a Justice of the Peace who never had a trial, and a doctor who rarely has a patient. Steamers now land goods at our doors, and the frequency of their visits will increase with our increasing numbers and wants.

Our inhabitants are moral, intelligent, progressive, and almost of cosmopolitan origin, consequently are broad and tolerant in their opinions and associations. * * * * We want more people, as that means better roads, more steamboats, more schools, bigger stores, more society, a higher civilization. There is room for many. The soil is a fine, light sandy loam with a clay subsoil. It produces sweet potatoes, cassava, conch and cow peas, sea island cotton, watermelons etc., abundantly. It responds with alacrity to the application of manure, and will then produce an immense variety of crops in perfection. * * * * The cost of provisions is about the same as in New England, but somewhat higher than in the Northwest. It costs much less here for rent, fuel and clothing than in either. Numerous men of liberal means are planting groves here, and this furnishes employment to such settlers as wish to labor for wages until their groves come into bearing. Wages for labor in the groves are $1.25 per day, mechanics proportionately higher. Choice five acre lots, suitable for groves and homes, can be bought for $75 to $200 each. It costs about $16 per acre to clear, $2.50 to plow, and 45 cents per rod for fence. Orange and lemon trees are from 25 to 75 cents each. * * * I can show a tree eleven years old from seed, thirty-nine inches around the trunk in the smallest place, which has borne $20 worth of oranges each year for two years. I can show others of the same age that never bore an orange. One grove near here of one-half an acre has brought the owner for fruit,

$1,200, $900, $1,500 for three years respectively. *Does it pay?* Come and see."

Route: By St. Johns river steamers to railroad at Astor. By railroad to Tavares on north shore of Lake Dora, thence by steamer to Tangerine.

A large hotel will be opened Oct. 1st. The "Tangerine Development Society" has issued a map of the locality with circular. Send stamp for it. Address,

J. H. FOSTER, Sec'y,
Tangerine, Orange County, Florida.

ZELLWOOD.

The western part of Orange county abounds in beautiful and attractive locations for making either permanent or winter homes. Particularly is this the case with the high ridge of open pine woods, extending southeast from Eustis, and on which are already situated the thriving and growing villages of Mount Dora, Tangerine, ZELLWOOD and Apopka.

ZELLWOOD located ten miles southeast of Lake Eustis, five miles from Lake Dora, and with the smaller lakes, Beauclaire, Carleton, Ola and Maggiore, in the immediate neighborhood, offers unexcelled attractions for homes, or for engaging in orange or other semi-tropical fruit culture. The country is high and rolling, timbered heavily with pine and free from undergrowth. The soil, underlaid with red clay, is better than average in quality, and its adaptability for growing oranges, lemons, limes, etc., is proven by many handsome and valuable groves in the vicinity.

The location is absolutely free from malaria, and its perfect healthfulness is shown in the immunity from sickness enjoyed by permanent residents from all parts of the North. Nowhere in Orange county can spots be found more free from all objectionable features, or that can be more readily, cheaply, and surely transformed into beautiful and healthful homes, or profitable orange groves.

The Tavares, Orlando & Atlantic Railroad, now in rapid process of construction, *will pass directly through Zellwood*, and give unbroken, all rail, Northern connections. This road, it is probable, will be completed within twelve months. At this time Zellwood is reached by private conveyance from Eustis, the terminus of the St. Johns & Lake Eustis Railroad.

Our place is laid out in five and ten acre lots for groves,

etc. For each lot we will give a building lot fronting on our lake, Maggiore. For terms apply to
J. A. WILLIAMSON, Agent.
Either of the undersigned will cheerfully give any further information personally or by letter.
J. A. WILLIAMSON,
R. G. ROBINSON.

ORANGE HEIGHTS.

This charming, delightful and healthful locality is two and one-half miles west of Apopka City and situated on Lake Apopka. It is one of the most healthful places to be found in all Florida, not even a case of yellow fever, sun stroke, or malaria has ever been known here. Situated as it is, back from the river on an elevation 175 feet above tide water, the atmosphere is perfectly dry, and the air cool and exhilarating. Some of the best young groves in the State are to be seen here and the soil is of the best in the county. The writer left Boston last winter, the first of February, seriously afflicted with catarrh and bronchitis. After consulting an eminent physician he was told that he could only find relief in Florida. He had coughed almost incessantly, and when he left Boston there were many doubts as to his recovery.

On the boat from Boston to Savannah he chanced to meet Mr. P. W. Swan, who was going to visit his son at Orange Heights; he kindly informed him of the healthfulness of the place and an invitation to call on him was cheerfully accepted.

The first impression on arriving at Orange Heights was of its lovely location; the second of its beautiful springs of clear, sparkling water. We have since had the water from the springs analyzed and found them to contain very healthful mineral properties. Had only been there a short time when coughing ceased, and in one month's time was entirely freed from catarrhal trouble.

Being favorably impressed with the place, decided to purchase land and set out a grove. Within the past year a number of New England people have become interested here and as they are showing considerable enterprise, building good frame houses and setting out some fine groves, we consider Orange Heights one of the best places in the county for newcomers to locate.

There is plenty of land to be had cheap, and a good neighborhood of honest, enterprising, church-going people.

It is on the line of the T., O. & A. R. R., and is south of latitude 29, thus insuring all kinds of vegetables from destructive frost.

On the pine land all kinds of the citrus family grow luxuriantly, and the hammock land of the Lake Apopka region is conceded by all to be the best in the State. If you want climate, health, good water, good rich soil cheap, and a good neighborhood on the line of a railroad, come to Orange Heights.

P. S.—An official analysis by our eminent State chemist has been printed of the properties of the mineral springs of Orange Heights, and will be sent free on application to Mr. E. C. Swan, at Orange Heights.

APOPKA.

For many years Apopka shared the fate of all South Florida towns. It was unheard of, an isolated hamlet, far beyond the borders of civilization, the only means of communication being the occasional steamers that plied the St. Johns, the nearest landing being at Melonville, near the present site of Sanford. Those were the days of the semi-monthly and weekly mails, when the pioneers of the piney woods ranged themselves along the counters of the solitary storeroom, in which the postoffice was located, and anxiously awaited the call of their names for letters from the old folks way up in New England, Georgia, the Carolinas and the far West. But things have changed. This state of affairs no longer exists, and we will, after a brief description of the Apopka region, note the difference between the Apopka of to-day and the obscure hamlet referred to above.

In 1854 an old couple named Rodgers settled upon a portion of the land now embraced in Apopka City. In 1855 Col. John L. Stewart and sons, and Peter Buchan and sons, moved from Georgia and cleared a considerable body of land. About 1860 Orange Lodge No. 36, F. & A. M., built a hall and for many years the place was known as the Lodge. For several years from 1868 to about 1870 the neighbors took turns to go weekly to Melonville, 22 miles distant, for the mail.

In 1868 the topography of the Apopka region attracted the attention of a physician, who desired to locate upon high, rolling land, as far removed as possible from swamps and other causes of disease. This gentleman was so well pleased with the location that he made it his home, and though "three score years and ten," is living to-day in better health than when he came, full of activity and enterprise, a monument to the wonderful salubrity of the climate and locality. All representation to the contrary, Apopka is one of the highest, if not the highest, location in the State of Florida. It is situated in township 21 south, of range 28 east; is 3½ miles south of the celebrated Clay Springs, which are the source of the Wekiva river, navigable for steamboats to the St. Johns (a distance of 18 miles), and is about the same distance west of the great Lake Apopka, next to Okeechobee, the largest body of water in the State.

Up to two years ago the progress made in developing this section was slow. The completion of the South Florida railroad, however, served as a stimulus, and resulted in at least doubling the number of inhabitants and buildings in Apopka. The surrounding country has been even more benefitted from the same cause.

The present population of Apopka and the immediate vicinity is about 800; increase within two years, 400. The rich hammocks and pine lands contiguous are being utilized rapidly for vegetable growing. The shipments last year aggregated several thousand crates, which realized fabulous prices in the Northern markets. Cucumbers, beans, onions, potatoes and tomatoes are the principal varieties raised. The number of orange trees in grove form within the corporate limits is nearly 11,000, and including the surrounding neighborhood, about double that number. These comprise groves in all stages of advancement, and count among the number some of the largest and most profitable in the county. There are, of course, many lemon and lime trees, and a constantly increasing variety of other fruits. Strawberry culture has not as yet been attempted beyond domestic needs. Pine apples are attracting attention as a crop that can be realized from in a short time, and their cultivation bids fair to rival that of the orange and other fruits.

A commodious and comfortable public school building is being erected, capable of accommodating 200 pupils. A competent and experienced principal has been selected, who will be assisted by a corps of efficient teachers.

The public buildings of Apopka are a town hall, masonic lodge, Methodist and Baptist churches. The membership of the Methodist church is about 75, Baptist 70, and the Presbyterians have a church organization with 22 members, but no edifice. The Episcopalians, also, have a church organization and monthly services. There are a drug store, several stores for general merchandizing, a hay and grain store, and a good livery stable with ample accommodations, all doing a fair and increasing business. It also has a weekly newspaper, the *Citizen*, and a live real estate agency, that of Davis & McKinney. Postal arrangements afford a money order office, a daily mail from the north, and a semi-weekly mail from a number of inter-county localities. Fresh beef of good quality and at low rates is furnished regularly from two to three times weekly. There are, also, two steam saw mills, two blacksmith and one wagon-making shop, and another saw mill will soon be in operation between Apopka and the lake.

The country around Apopka is high and rolling, covered with a heavy growth of yellow and pitch pine. The timber is simply magnificent. The whole region is interspersed with beautiful, clear water lakes, full of the finest fish, affording the rarest sport and an excellent diet. The quality of the land is not surpassed by any other section of the famed Orange county. Almost every foot of it is suitable for orange culture, and many orange groves in the bearing stage can be pointed out that have been made without the use of fertilizers. Besides the pine lands, there are a number of tracts of high hammocks, of the richest quality of soil, covered with hickory, oak, magnolia, sweet gum, bay, and the wild orange and palmetto. This grade of land is unsurpassed in the United States for natural fertility and adaptability to gardening purposes, besides the growth of the orange, which it frequently brings into bearing in from five to seven years from the seed. The great hammocks along the eastern shore of Lake Apopka, alone insure the future prosperity of this section, comprising, as they do, hundreds of acres of the finest vegetable land in the world, protected from damaging frost from the north and west by 150 square miles of water never at a lower temperature than 60 deg. fah., over which cold winds must pass to reach them.

THE ORLANDO, TAVARES & ATLANTIC RAILROAD.

Apopka is located directly on the line of the Orlando, Tavares & Atlantic Railroad, which connects with the Transit railroad at Leesburg, forming a direct, all-rail route with the North. This road will prove the most formidable competition the St. Johns river has yet had in securing the carrying trade of South Florida. Work has been going on actively for several months in grading from Tavares toward Orlando, and Apopka being midway between these points will probably have been reached by the graders and ironers when these pages come from the press. It is expected that the whole line will be in operation by the 1st of January, 1884.

Independently of railroad communication, Apopka enjoys the advantage of water transportation by the way of the Wekiva river. For years past this river has been navigated by steamboats and barges up to its source, Clay Springs. These springs, within 3½ miles of Apopka, are destined to become famous as a resort for invalids and pleasure seekers from all parts. The waters are strongly, though not repugnantly, impregnated with sulphur and other medicinals, and have a reputation for effecting remarkable cures of scrofulous diseases.

A candid comprehension of the advantages offered by the Apopka region must inevitably lead to the conclusion that, all things considered, it is one of the most favored sections of South Florida, and that, therefore, the homeseeker, the healthseeker, or the tourist will find it both profitable and pleasant to pay it a visit. The hospitable character of its inhabitants, from all parts of the Union, warmed up with the prospects of a brilliant future, will insure them a kindly greeting and outstretched hands.

THE APOPKA REAL ESTATE AND LOAN AGENCY.
DAVIS & MCKINNEY.

This agency is the livest feature of the Apopka region. It has been in existence but a few months, yet has exerted a marked influence in attracting the attention of settlers to the country. Both members of the firm are young men full of energy and perseverance, and are determined that the outside world shall not lack intelligence of the beautiful country they operate in. Messrs. Davis & McKinney hold contracts, and are sale agents for the sale of upwards of $200,000 worth of the choicest orange groves and unimproved lands in their section. With but few exceptions, the valuations on this property are the same as fixed upon it twelve months ago, and previous to the commencement of active operations on the Tavares, Orlando & Atlantic Railroad. Hardly one of the groves on their list could be made at a less cost than the price at which it is held. The cause of this has been lack of transportation. But with the now assured railroad prospects, the opportunities for immediate paying investment in the Apopka section are obvious. The experience of other localities that have been tapped by the iron horse will undoubtedly be reenacted in the case of Apopka.

Messrs. Davis & McKinney have teams in constant readiness, and will cheerfully conduct prospective settlers through the Apopka region free of charge. Both members of the firm are well known throughout Orange county, do not exaggerate the advantages of the country, and make it a rule never to importune those who call on them to buy against their will and judgment. They unhesitatingly refer to all persons of prominence in the county, and those who have had business dealings with them. Correspondence solicited.

THE SOUTH FLORIDA CITIZEN

Was established in April, 1879, by Rev. W. M. and A. M. C. Russell. Rev. F. A. Taylor, A. M., is the present editor and proprietor. A new press and outfit have recently been purchased and the paper will hereafter be called the *Apopka Citizen*. It will be a reliable local newspaper, devoted to the interests of Apopka City, Orange county and Florida. Terms $1.50 per annum in advance.

OCOEE.

This is a little village of about a dozen families, one store, postoffice, school, steam saw mill, etc., located on Starke Lake, two and a half miles south of Lake Apopka. One of the many embryo towns in the county.

The following are a few of the inducements it offers. There has never a case of chills originated at the place, and the healthfulness and water cannot be surpassed in the county. Some of the richest lands in the county, pine and hammock, are in this locality and cheaper than any other place, other advantages being equal. Insects are not troublesome, some families never putting up a mosquito net the year round. Hunting and fishing are not surpassed. The water protection against cold is better than at any other locality in the county; we seldom have the tenderest vegetable or small fruits killed by frost when they have been killed all around us. Some of the finest bearing groves in the county are in this vicinity, and more vegetables are raised for market. There are a number of beautiful young groves in this settlement for sale reasonably. Want of transportation has been the only drawback, but before this pamphlet is out we will have daily communication with Jacksonville.

The people of Ocoee and vicinity are enterprising, moral and intelligent. Each one seems to be too much engrossed in his own affairs, and too well satisfied with the success which attends his efforts, to allow any feelings of malice or envy to exist in his mind. There are no neighborhood quarrels. Justices of the peace have few or no official duties, a busy, thriving people, all rejoicing in the general prosperity of a section, and all confident that this particular locality, when fully developed, will be one of the richest and most attractive to be found anywhere, bear nothing but good will toward each other. Such communities naturally attract strangers, and secure the best citizens from coming immigration.

This is Ocoee society. A fertile, agricultural and fruit growing region surrounds the embryo town. Gardening and truck farming are extensively and profitably carried on. With the opening of the Apopka canal to navigation the increased transportation facilities have given a fresh impetus to this industry, and the coming winter will show more extensive operations and greater profits.

For particulars address the postmaster at Ocoee, with stamp, who will be pleased to give you all the information you want.

GOTHA.

This beautiful town, situated on the shores of Lake Olivia and several smaller lakes, is about eight miles due west of Orlando and has an elevation of 200 or more feet above tide water, being on the back bone of Florida. The lands are the choicest, rolling high pine, and a pleasant, cool breeze continually prevails. It is remarkably free from insect pests, malarial and other diseases. The lovely Lake Olivia is from 20 to 30 feet deep, the waters pure and limpid and the shores of clean, white sand, while the banks slope gradually all around giving excellent building sites for hundreds of families.

Here, after traveling all over Florida, Mr. H. A. Hempel, (the inventor of the celebrated Hempel Quoin for printers, from which he derives a handsome income,) decided to make a home, feeling sure that the many advantages of the location would attract a goodly number of people of a social and progressive disposition like himself. He, therefore, secured a thousand acres of this choice land besides a tract on Apopka Lake four miles distant.

Lumber was needed, hence he built a fine saw, shingle and planing mill, the finest and most complete in this section. With the lumber from the mill he has built several handsome houses, a fine store, etc., and settlers come in and commence their improvements. The public school commenced Oct. 1st.

Mr. Hempel has a fine grove of young orange trees and a variety of fruits besides quite a number of acres of peas, potatoes, vegetables, etc. Around his houses are fine tracts of Bermuda grass, and everything shows vigorous growth.

He employs intelligent and competent men on his own place and to care for the groves of others who are unable to spend the whole year here, charging them only the actual cost.

The tract of land is laid out in village lots, residence lots, and garden and farm lots. Also a number of choice locations on Lake Olivia for winter homes for Northerners.

A charter has been obtained for a railroad that is to run through this tract of land from Orlando, and the Jacksonville, Tampa & Key West Railroad, now in course of rapid construction, will pass near Lake Apopka and within a couple of miles of Gotha, and possibly through the village. Mr. Hempel will soon build a dock on Lake Apopka, from and through which there is an all-water route to the St. Johns river, thus giving in the near future several routes of transportation. At present Gotha is reached through Orlando, from which place there is a regular mail, and from whence conveyances may be had to visit this exceedingly healthful and interesting section of country.

LAKE WANEE AND SURROUNDINGS.

Six miles west of the flourishing town of Orlando, the county seat of Orange county, and situated in townships 22 and 23 south, range 28 east, is to be found one of the most desirable locations in South Florida, and why such a fine section should have escaped the grasp of those desiring lands for speculation, is a mystery the writer is unable to solve. But such is the case, and the lands are principally owned by young, hard working white men, who are willing to divide their lands up with those seeking homes, at very low figures in order to have neighbors. There are yet some desirable Government lands to be had, and the writer will take pleasure in showing them up to parties desiring to settle among us. We do not propose to act selfishly. We want all the working men we can get to come among us and help develop a settlement, every acre of which will be a small fortune to the owners in a few years. We have a large variety of lands, and if you do not wish to engage in orange culture you can follow other pursuits. We have lands admirably adapted to truck farming; in fact any crops raised in the United States can be successfully grown here. I will give a brief description of the lands, confining myself to this particular section.

The lands, as a general thing, are what may be termed No. 1 pine, while at the same time they are well elevated, being about 100 feet higher than the lands at Sanford on the

St. Johns river, only a distance of twenty-two miles. The country for four or five miles around is high and rolling, the principal growth being pine and turkey-oak. Beautiful clear water lakes filled with fine fish are to be seen in every direction, and the much coveted lake fronts are to be had on almost every quarter section. The Hon. A. B. Longaker, of Allentown, Pa., after traveling over the entire State of Florida and locating for himself and friends over 9,000 acres of land, returned to this section and located for himself a quarter section on a beautiful little lake, where he proposes to build for himself a home for his old age. As yet Orlando is our nearest point to transportation, but we have three chances for transportation at our very doors at an early date. The Tampa & Key West Railroad survey passes near us, and a company has been formed and a charter granted for a railroad from Orlando to Oakland, Fla., which will pass directly through this settlement. Boats are already running from South Apopka to Tavares, and dredging will commence from Apopka to Butler at an early date, which will give us close communication by water. Some substantial improvements are going on already. Some of the parties whom I will name as being among the principal land holders on Lake Wanee:

D. C. Clem, of Linville, Va., 160 acres; Joseph Blanc, 160 acres, 5 acre grove; Eugene E. Pope, 160 acres, 5 acre grove; N. J. Lewis, 160 acres, J. S. Tyler, 120 acres; L. G. Harper, 320 acres, 10 acre grove; William Powell, 80 acres, 10 acre grove; J. E. Holeman, 40 acres; J. J. Davis, 40 acres, 5 acre grove.

Some choice lands are to be found on Lake Hiwassee. This fine sheet of water lies north of Wanee, and is only divided by a narrow strip of land of a few acres. The principal owners of land and groves on this lake are J. M. McConnell; J. M. Austin, 200 acres, 10 acre grove; J. D. Newsome, 100 acres, 6 acres grove; Homer Duke, 20 acres; J. N. Wilson, 40 acres; C. F. Hancock, 200 acres, 5 acre grove; Willis N. Parker, 240 acres; J. O. Sessoms, 160 acres, improvements; George B. Pope, 160 acres, improvements; Hiram Beasly, 40 acres, improvements.

Improvements are rapidly making their appearance in this vicinity, and will at an early date make a large and prosperous settlement. One mile northwest of Lake Hiwassee, and immediately on the mail route from Orlando to Sumterville, quite a settlement is rapidly forming and some substantial improvements are booming up on the banks of Lake May, which, by the way, is one of the prettiest lakes in Florida. On the south of this lake Dr. Griffin, formerly of Atlanta, Ga., has erected a grist and saw mill, which is driven by a Turbine wheel, with a fall of twenty feet of water from a lake above Lake May. E. W. Speir, postmaster at Orlando, and Messrs. Argue & Carpenter, of Washington, D. C., own fine property on the east side of this lake and are planting out a ten acre grove, and anticipate adding to it until forty acres or more are completed. On the north W. H. McGwigan has a quarter section with comfortable dwelling on it. He has a fine lake view and several beautiful building spots. He anticipates planting a large grove at an early date.

There are many others making improvements and owning lands that I have not mentioned, as my object was only to show a few of the principal land owners. Parties wishing to make a home in Florida, or those desiring to make solid investments will find it to their interest to communicate or call on me before making purchases elsewhere. I will obligate to furnish good orange and vegetable lands at from $3 to $15 per acre. I have the management of several fine bodies of land that belong to parties at a distance, that can be bought at figures that will double themselves in six months. Lands will be bought, cleared, set in orange trees and cared for for parties living at a distance, who cannot superintend the work themselves. All communications should be addressed to L. G. HARPER,
Orlando, Orange Co., Fla.

THE LAKE WORONOCO REGION.

Ten miles northeast of Orlando, six miles due east of Winter Park and three miles south of east from Lake Howell, is the beautiful Lake Woronoco. The country is rolling and covered with a fine growth of pine, while numerous lovely, clear water lakes diversify the scene and their banks afford excellent building sites. There are no Government lands here and but few improved places, it being almost a *terra incognita* less than two years ago. Its natural beauty and the excellence of its lands for orange growing are now, however, attracting much attention and several families are expected to locate there the present season, though the lands are held at $10 and upward per acre. It is on the projected line of the Tavares, Orlando & Atlantic railroad, and will in a few years undoubtedly be greatly developed and a thriving social center, with all the appurtenances of modern civilization, as its only need is more people imbued with the

desire to make for themselves pleasant homes in this lovely and healthful region. For further particulars address, with stamps, SHERMAN ADAMS,
Orlando, Florida.

THE SOUTH FLORIDA RAILROAD.

A very important factor in the wonderfully rapid development of that beautiful section of country in the very heart of the Orange Belt, southwesterly from Sanford, is the South Florida Railroad, under the able management of its wide awake and efficient president, Mr. J. E. Ingraham, to whose energy of character and marked business ability is due much of the remarkable success which has characterized this important enterprise.

To Mr. B. R. Swoope, the superintendent, and Mr. F. H. Rand, the general freight and passenger agent, are also due a full meed of praise, and those who are acquainted with the scope and character of their work, know that the interests of the road are safe and progressive in their capable hands. Nor must we forget Dr. C. C. Haskell, the treasurer, and one of the original incorporators, a very energetic and courteous gentleman, without whose aid the road would not have been built. In fact all connected with the road seem to be overflowing with energy, enterprise and wise foresight.

The history of the road may be briefly stated as follows: In the heart of Orange county was a lovely and productive country awaiting development. Mr. E. W. Henck of Longwood, and Dr. C. C. Haskell, of Maitland, realized that the time had come for action in place of the talk in which others were indulging. They associated with themselves Messrs. A. Meuser and E. T. Crafts and procured articles of incorporation, which were advertised in June, 1879, and in October they secured a charter for a railroad from the St. Johns river to Charlotte Harbor on the Gulf of Mexico, with a capital of $120,000. Survey work commenced in November, and January 10, 1880, a great celebration was held at Sanford, many distinguished men being present, and General Grant inaugurated the enterprise by digging the first spadefull of earth, and work commenced in earnest. In the meantime the Boston (Mass.) *Daily Herald*, by its able owners and managers, Mr. R. M. Pulsifer and Mr. E. B. Haskell, the latter a brother of Dr. H., had become interested and provided the bulk of the capital for the enterprise, and the road has often been noted as the first and only one built, owned and run by a newspaper.

They perfected their organization January 29, 1880, electing the following officers: President, E. W. Henck; Treasurer, Dr. C. C. Haskell; Secretary, E. T. Crafts; Chief Engineer, F. C. Tucker, and the organizers as directors. January 29, 1881, Mr. J. E. Ingraham was elected President; Dr. C. C. Haskell, Treasurer; E. T. Crafts, Secretary; E. R. Trafford, Chief Engineer, and the following Board of Directors: J. E. Ingraham, B. R. Swoope, Dr. C. C. Haskell, E. R. Trafford and E. T. Crafts, also B. R. Swoope as Superintendent and F. H. Rand as General Freight and Passenger Agent. In August Mr. Crafts resigned, and Mr. F. H. Rand was elected to fill the vacancy. The same persons were re-elected in 1882 and in 1883. Mr. Trafford, however, retired early this year to give his whole attention to the interests of the Sanford Grant, which is developing very rapidly under his able management.

So vigorously was the work prosecuted, that by June 1, 1880, the road was in operation to Longwood, July 1st to Maitland, and December 1st to Orlando. The business done far exceeded the most sanguine expectations, and has steadily increased year by year, one surprising feature being the fact that the business of each succeeding summer has exceeded that of the preceding winter, proving beyond question the solid and rapid growth of the country.

In June, 1881, an extension was surveyed from Orlando to Kissimmee City; the work commenced in July, and the road opened for business in March, 1882. During the summer a charter was obtained extending the road to Tampa, the route surveyed and a force of 1,200 to 1,500 men employed, the Plant railroad Syndicate taking a three-fifths interest in the road. So great is the energy displayed that the road is expected to be open to the public early in January, 1884. It is being built in a very substantial manner and the equipment is to be first-class in every respect. The track is laid with forty pound steel rails, using Wharton's improved safety switches, Mason's improved engines with extended smoke box to secure passengers from all annoyance by smoke or cinders. Each through train will have a fine drawing-room car, as well as elegant passenger coaches, smoking-car, mail, baggage and express cars, etc. In fact nothing will be spared that will conduce to the comfort, safety and convenience of the passengers.

This extension of the road will aid greatly in the development of the country, and thousands will pass over the line that otherwise would stay away. The company have very fine lands along the line of the road, which will be sold at very reasonable rates, and they are giving particular attention to the development of special localities.

The names of the stations are: SANFORD R. R. WHARF, SANFORD, BELAIR, CRYSTAL LAKE, BENT'S, LONGWOOD, SNOW'S, MAYO, MAITLAND, WINTER PARK, WILLCOX, ORLANDO, PINE CASTLE, MCKINNON, KISSIMMEE, FT. DAVENPORT, HORSE CREEK, BARTOW, MADORA, SHILO, TAMPA. .

At Sanford the Company have a very fine depot, and commodious and substantial freight houses; also at several other points on the line, and new ones are being steadily built, the intention being to give every place a handsome depot, etc. At Sanford are the Company's offices and general headquarters, also their extensive car and machine shops, which are turning out excellent and substantial work. The hundredth part has not been said, but space forbids further mention.

THE FLORIDA LAND AND COLONIZATION COMPANY.

This organization has its headquarters at Sanford, though their interests extend over a large part of the State in Orange, Polk, Hernando, Brevard, Sumter, Alachua and Marion counties, all choice selections located several years ago and unquestionably among the best lands in the State. They offer land for sale in lots to suit purchasers at moderate prices, varying according to location and quality, on easy terms to actual settlers. This company purchased Hon. H. S. Sanford's interest in the Sanford Grant, a fine body of land on the south side of Lake Munroe, and have laid out a large amount of money in building streets, wharves, hotels, water works, gas and planting shade trees. The Sanford Grant was an old Spanish interest, confirmed under treaty with Spain by the United States Supreme Court, and consequently has a perfect title. It embraces twenty-five square miles of territory at the head of navigation on the St. Johns river, latitude 28 degrees, 50 minutes north. This section is now recognized as among the best in the State for the cultivation of semi-tropical fruits, especially oranges and lemons, owing to its exemption from injurious frosts, accessibility to market and facilities of transportation.

At the State Fair at Jacksonville on the 25th of January, 1881, the first prizes were given to pine apples, lemons, limes, lemon and citron blossoms, cabbage, cauliflowers, turnips, etc., from Sanford, in all nine premiums for the Grant, a unique exhibit after the frost which did so much damage in other regions.

There are a large number of orange groves on the Grant and adjoining, one of which 30 years old, yields an annual income of from $2,000 to $3,000 from 250 trees. The Speer grove, near Sanford, from four and a half acres has averaged $4,500 for the past eleven years, one year yielding $7,300 nett.

The land on the lake is generally low, with pine, deciduous cypress, and cabbage-palm trees; it rises gradually as it recedes from the lake, into high, rolling land, of light, apparently sandy soil, covered with yellow pine trees, interspersed with "blackjack," and occasional hammock of hard timber, which gives the richest known soil, the whole dotted with beautiful, deep, clear water lakes of spring water. Muck is abundant, and very valuable for fertilizing purposes. The lands of the Grant are especially desirable to those wishing to plant orange or lemon groves, as offering special attractions in the facilities near at hand—churches, schools, transportation, daily mail, express, telegraph, printing office, railroad shops, etc., all being within easy reach, and living expenses, therefore, greatly reduced and comfort increased.

It is proposed to utilize the new Swedes colony, which landed here in November last, in establishing at once 25 five-acre groves, to be offered for sale, and also through the same reliable labor, to have them cared for on contract for one or a term of years; the usual price per acre and per annum for care of a grove, once established, is $20. Non-residents can have lands selected for them on the Grant, cleared, fenced, and planted with choice imported stock (from Belair if desired,) to order, and can depend upon good selections, good work, and thorough management. There are fine groves on the Grant so conducted, owned by prominent citizens of the North, since years, and not yet seen by their owners. The old Swedes colony make a specialty of caring for orange groves, and their own groves (many of which are for sale,) give evidence of their skill and care in the business they have followed for twelve years past. Such opportunities to secure with little trouble and small cost, in perhaps the most eligible position in Florida, winter homes, orange, mandarin and lemon groves, and pineapple plantations, are, probably, not to be found elsewhere, and when one reflects that it will cost $50 per acre to transport a full orange crop five miles, the advantage of close proximity to attain transportion will be appreciated. The price of clearing land per acre, is about

$20; trees are planted from 70 to 100 to the acre. Nursery stock suitable for planting young groves can be bought, unbudded at from $25 to $50 per hundred, according to size and age; budded from $50 to $100 per hundred. The price of labor is from $15 to $20 per month with board; beef 7c to 10c per pound; flour about $1 per bbl. above New York prices, and so relatively for other imported provisions and groceries; fish and game plentiful, and very cheap.

The new town of McKinnon on the South Florida Railroad was laid out during the summer of 1883, and now has a store, saw mill, postoffice, etc., besides having twenty or more groves started. This place is an elevation in the flat woods of remarkably good land, good water, few insects and being high and dry must be healthy. Land heretofore has been sold in this town at a very low price for immediate improvement, no lots being sold to speculators. It is proposed to erect a church this coming winter. Being located on the railroad, transportation of course will be good.

The other property belonging to this company is scattered throughout the counties mentioned, among which is a body of land lying on and near Lake Apopka, consisting of pine and hammock; Gardener's Island on the Kissimmee river; Anclote, in Hernando county, where there is some recently drained, rich saw-grass land, suitable for sugar cane. A fine body of land in Alachua county, etc.

When the Florida Land and Colonization Company purchased the Hon. Mr. Sanford's interest there had been but comparatively little done toward improving the property. Lands had been sold and groves made and brought into bearing, but no system of drainage for the flat woods and grass ponds. Under its present management it is proposed to drain many spots of rich land which are now useless on account of occasional flooding during heavy rains, and thus open up some of the best and richest cane and garden lands in the country.

Pine apples, guavas, Japan persimmons, and other like perishable fruit, has been sent from here to New York and arrived in prime condition. Beans, tomatoes, Irish potatoes, and other vegetables were shipped in quantities during last March, April and May, and very satisfactory prices received; some potatoes shipped during April bringing from seven to nine dollars a barrel; beans selling for three dollars per bushel crate, close connections and quick transportation putting the vegetables into New York City within five days.

Mr. E. R. Trafford, Sanford, Florida, is the agent for this company.

DISSTON PURCHASE—4,000,000 ACRES.

FLORIDA LAND AND IMPROVEMENT COMPANY.

Hamilton Disston, Pres. | T. Henry Asbury, Treas.
J. J. Dunne, Vice Pres. | Richard Salinger, Sec'y.
W. T. Forbes, Land Commissioner.

Have still in Orange county about 90,000 acres which they offer for sale generally in blocks of 80 acres or more at $1.25 per acre.

Lands within six miles of railroad or steamer transportation are graded at $2.50 per acre.

Their lands include every variety of upland and lowland, and are adapted to oranges, lemons, limes, pineapples, bananas, sugar cane, early vegetables, etc., and are situated chiefly in the counties of Duval, St. Johns, Volusia, Brevard, Orange, Sumter, Levy, Alachua, Hernando, Hillsborough, Polk, Manatee and Monroe.

Apply for information or purchase to R. H. Marks, agent, Sanford, Fla., or to the general office of the company at Jacksonville.

W. T. Forbes,
Land Com. Jacksonville, Fla.

KISSIMMEE LAND COMPANY.

T. Henry Asbury, Pres. | W. T. Forbes, Manager.
Hamilton Disston, Vice Pres. | L. W. Klahr, Treas.
T. W. Palmer, Secretary.

Principal office, Jacksonville, Fla. Branch office, Kissimmee City, Fla.

Owns and has for sale a large portion of Kissimmee City, and the whole of the Florida L. & I. Co.'s addition to that flourishing town.

The town of Kissimmee is situated at the head of navigation of the Kissimmee and Caloosahatchee rivers, and has direct water communication through these streams and Lake Okeechobee to the Gulf of Mexico. It has also railroad transportation northward, and in a few weeks from the issuing of this pamphlet will have railroad communication with Tampa on the Gulf coast.

The Company, after a year of careful inspection, has selected and purchased about 200,000 acres of land in Orange, Brevard, Polk, Hillsborough, and Monroe counties; also smaller tracts in Hernando, Sumter and Duval counties.

These lands are among the most desirable in the State, both for residence and culture of oranges and other fruits and vegetables, and are readily accessible by either present or prospective railroad and steamer routes.

They were carefully selected by thoroughly competent judges of Florida land, especially for their adaptability to the culture of vegetables and semi-tropical fruits.

We offer them for sale in quantities to suit purchasers at from $2.50 to $10 per acre, according to quality and location. Address.

W. T. FORBES, Manager,
Jacksonville, Florida.

OKEECHOBEE LAND COMPANY.

The lands of this Company in the Kissimmee and Caloosahatchee valleys, are now for sale at graded prices.

These lands are a portion of the large body which lies in the fertile valleys of the two streams mentioned. It is the opinion of competent persons who have examined them, that they will soon become the most productive sugar lands on the Continent. The attention of capitalists is already attracted to them, and the time is close at hand when extensive sugar plantations will be flourishing throughout these valleys.

There are also fine orange lands here, while the situation so far south insures safety against frost for the most sensitive of the tropical and semi-tropical fruits.

Apply to W. T. FORBES, Land Com'r,
Jacksonville, Fla.

SANFORD.

The town of Sanford was founded about the year 1872, but its material prosperity may be dated from the building of the Sanford House, which was opened to the public on the 6th of January, 1876. Up to that time the place contained a dry goods and grocery store, drug store and postoffice, printing office, saw mill, Episcopal church, two residences and, wharf. Witness the change of eight years. Now it has a city government and embraces within its corporate limits, nearly one thousand souls, and the following business resume: Four mammoth general merchandise stores, five groceries, two drug stores, vegetable store, bazaar of fashion, dry goods and clothing store, saddle and harness shop, hardware store, two sash, door, blind and paint stores, two furniture stores, two wagon shops, two merchant tailors, newspaper and job office, bank, jewelry and curiosity store, two restaurants, vegetable store, bakery, soda bottling establishment, two livery stables, three hotels, four or five boarding houses, mammoth saw mill, two barber shops, dental office, orange packing house, four law offices, four physicians, two land agencies, door, sash, blind and scroll work manufactory, sportsmen's outfitting establishment, and various other small industries. Beside these, the car works and machine shops of the South Florida Railroad are located here, which furnish employment for a large number of men. The Episcopal, Presbyterian, and Methodist denominations have each a neat house of worship, and the public school is attended by over 100 pupils.

Sanford is located 200 miles south of Jacksonville, on the south margin of Lake Monroe, a beautiful sheet of water five by seven miles in extent, through which the noble St. Johns river flows. The town is situated on land that rises to an elevation of 25 feet above the lake, thus rendering it susceptible of the best drainage, and insuring its health.

The town is supplied with water by the Sanford Water Works Co., which brings the water from a large, clear water lake three miles distant, which water works is used by the fire department in case of fire.

This is virtually the head of navigation for large steamers, and we have, during the winter (or orange) season some thirty-five arrivals and departures of steamers weekly. As a commercial point Sanford has no equal in the State, except Jacksonville, Fernandina and Pensacola. Small steamers run from here to the famous Indian river country, and the South Florida Railroad, now running from here to Kissimmee, the fountain head of all the great Lake Okeechobee region, will soon be completed to Tampa, which will make this road the great thoroughfare for tourists and traffic to Cuba and Havana. With all these advantages, the town has a bright future before it.

Through various sources the town has already acquired a wide fame. First, through the influence and liberality of its founder, Hon. H. S. Sanford, formerly U. S. Minister to Belgium. Second, through the visit of Gens. U. S. Grant and Sheridan, some three years since, when Grant turned the first shovel of dirt on the South Florida railroad. Third, through the visit of President Arthur and party, last spring, who spent a delightful period at the Sanford House. As a business point, and for a winter resort it has no superior in the State.

CAPT. RICHARD H. MARKS.

Capt. Richard H. Marks, of the Orange County Land Agency, with headquarters at Sanford, came to Orange county fifteen years ago and is probably as well posted about Florida lands as any man in the county. He certainly ought to be, as his facilities have certainly been splendid. He also knows how to make an orange grove. As proof of this he has made the finest one hundred acre grove in the county, and he is now offering to sell it for $125,000. He is handling a great many fine orange groves on commission and claims that no other agent can offer better bargains than he can. He is agent for the Florida Land and Improvement Company in this county. He also has a fine selection of U. S. Lands which he offers to enter for $2 per acre. These lands are not in Orange county, but in Polk and Hernando counties.

He has on his books, for sale, a very large and well assorted list of properties of all kinds: orange groves, orange lands, town lots in Sanford and Kissimmee and at other points along the railroad. He invites anyone coming to

Florida to give him a call, and feels confident that he will be able to render assistance in making selections.

He charges nothing for showing you property, and if he cannot show you what you want he does not ask you to buy.

He claims to have sold more land during the last twelve months than any other agent in the county, and he makes it a rule to try to sell you just what he thinks will suit you, as he claims that it does not pay him to sell a man property that he will be dissatisfied with. The best friends he has are men who have bought property through his agency. His office is centrally located in Sanford, corner Palmetto Avenue and First Street, where he will be glad to meet any one interested in Florida. He is getting out a new list of "properties for sale," which he will mail to all applicants.

J. J. BUCHHEIT'S
DINING ROOMS AND HOTEL

On Palmetto street are the headquarters for those desiring the best of eatables, cooked to perfection and served in an artistic manner for a very moderate price. Mr. Buchheit is an experienced and accomplished restaurantier, and those who are so fortunate as to partake of the excellent fare he provides will not go away disappointed, but will return at the first opportunity.

The papers of this section pronounce his place the "Delmonico" of the South, and we judge the compliment to be well deserved, the bill of fare, style of cooking, etc., being well calculated to please. His hotel is centrally situated at Sanford and easy of access from depot and steamboat landings. Rooms are furnished if desired.

CAPT. J. Z. McDONALD.

The estate of the genial Capt. McD. comprises some 600 acres of the best land in this section of the country, just north of Longwood, which is his postoffice. Born in Buffalo, N. Y., he came here from Ohio in 1874, and took up a fine homestead to which he has since added by purchase. Then the country was a wilderness. He now has twenty-four acres of orange groves—some bearing—a very pleasant and deliciously comfortable house. The yard is covered with vigorous Bermuda grass, dotted here and there with fine trees and beautiful flowers, that attract the attention of the passengers as the cars of the South Florida Railroad pause at the station and give rise to exclamations of delight.

Two-thirds of his choice location are fine bottom lands, lying both sides of Soldier creek in its circuitous course. The balance is rolling, high pine land. These bottom lands are the natural home of the orange, and the wild sour and bitter sweet oranges found growing here have been transplanted over a large extent of the surrounding country. The other native trees are cabbage palm, gum trees, tuber, sweet and black ; hickory, native poplar, whitewood or tulip, bass wood, oak—live, water, white, turkey and post ; ironwood, cedar, cypress, elm ; white, red and magnolia bay ; ash, mulberry of large size, wild orange, buckeye, or horse chestnut, sweet elder, very large, etc., etc. Here, too, is an immense cypress tree, the largest probably in South Florida, fourteen feet eight inches in diameter near the ground, and estimated to be ten feet through at eighty feet altitude. Near by are immense whitewood trees that would attract attention were they not dwarfed by this giant.

Capt. McDonald proposes to sell either high pine or bottom lands to actual settlers in quantities to suit at moderate prices, and gives an excellent opportunity to those desiring to raise groves or vegetable gardens, as he has lands peculiarly adapted to either, or both, as may be seen from what he has accomplished. Those desiring a home should investigate the inducements he offers.

LONGWOOD.

Longwood is located nine and one-half miles from Sanford, and is the first station of importance on the South Florida Railroad after leaving the latter place. The elevation is seventy-six feet above Lake Monroe ; the country is perfectly healthy the year round, and, though inclining to be flat where the village is located, the general character of the land is high, rolling pine of the first quality, heavily timbered and interspersed with beautiful clear water lakes. It is not claimed that our lands are any better than those of our neighbors, but as good, and there are more acres of first quality orange lands tributary to Longwood than to any other place on the South Florida Railroad. This country is thickly settled by a well-to-do and educated class, making the village one of the best places for business in the State.

Longwood was first settled in 1873, by Mr. E. W. Henck, of Boston, the projector and first President of the South Florida Railroad. He was soon followed by Julius Molnar, a young Hungarian, who was without means, but who, by push, energy and indomitable will, has made one of the finest orange groves in the county, and he is not only the owner of this valuable property, but is the foremost merchant of the town, carrying as heavy and fine a stock of general merchandize as can be found in any of the towns of South Florida.

The next settler was J. N. Tearcy, of Tennessee, who starting without capital has raised a fine orange grove and is one of our solid men. A. Meuser, a German, also without means, came in 1874. He has been one of the ablest and most helpful of the promoters of our town; he was one of the original directors of the South Florida Railroad, and the hardest worker in making that road a success. The most unswerving integrity and unusual pluck and push have made him one of our foremost citizens. Mr. J. H. Wooldridge, of Kentucky, has also become a successful merchant; he was one of our original settlers and started at the bottom. We mention these gentlemen as evidence that men of the right stuff can start in this country without money and succeed. Our other merchants are Mr. C. V. S. Wilson, general merchandise; A. W. Thompson, grocery, restaurant and boarding-house; Edward Molnar, bakery; J. L. Ball, hay and grain; F. Holborn, jeweler; Mrs. Holborn, millinery; H. Hemingway, drugs; T. Griggs, butcher; John Stewart, restaurant. Of course we have a billiard room. A hardware store is much needed, and several boarding houses would do a thriving business, as Longwood is the point of departure for passengers and mails to Altamonte and Apopka. Our physicians are Dr. H. Hemingway, (allopathic,) late of London, England, and Dr. Charles E. Walker, (homeopathic,) late of Natick, Mass., both gentlemen of large experience and successful practice.

Our chief industry is a sash, door and blind factory and saw mill, the only establishment of the kind in the State. Everything requisite for building a house is turned out at this factory, and machinery for making furniture is to be added at once. The fine mantels, panel work and doors, made from our beautiful Florida woods, are already becoming famous. This enterprise is owned and conducted by Mr. P. A. Demens, whose energy is doing wonders for this section of the county. Mr. Demens will add an ice factory the coming winter.

A fine wagon and blacksmith shop is owned by Henry Hand, whose fine work is becoming widely known. Other manufactories will probably soon follow, as land is offered free to all enterprises of any nature that will benefit the town.

Carpenters and other workingmen are in great demand. Sash and door makers and other wood workers are being added constantly to the force in our factory. Any man willing to work can find employment here at good wages.

Regular services are held in a neat Episcopal church. The colored people have a Baptist church and are about to erect a school house. The Presbyterians, Baptists and Methodists also hold weekly services. The school house for white children is one of the finest in South Florida, and our school well taught and well attended. Our society is the best from North, South, East and West, and the stranger, no matter whence he comes, will find some one here from his home place or its immediate vicinity.

The necessary steps have been taken to obtain a local government, and Longwood will, on December 3d, 1883, become an incorporated town, when sidewalks will be laid, shade trees planted, and the streets improved. We shall then strive to earn the name of being the thriftiest and cleanest town in South Florida.

Longwood, already noted for its excellent water and general healthfulness, offers in its immediate vicinity the finest of orange lands at prices which defy competition. We offer low prices with the best facilities in transportation, there being but ten miles of rail to the St. Johns river, whence traffic is cheap and speedy; we offer the finest school and church facilities and daily mail and telegraph; we offer health to the invalid and the best of sport to the sportsman; we offer cheap homes and steady work to the workingman, good opportunities to business men, and superior investments to capitalists. Though we have no regular land agent here, strangers will find a hearty welcome and those who will willingly give them every facility for seeing the country without expense. Letters enclosing stamp and addressed to E. W. Henck & Co., will be promptly and cheerfully answered.

ALTAMONTE.

Altamonte is located ten miles north of Orlando, thirteen miles southwest of Sanford and two miles west of Snow's station on the South Florida Railroad, on beautiful, high, rolling pine land, with now and then a little rich hammock. It has for special attractions the famous Hoosier and Shepherd Springs, and charming Lake Brantley. The soil is generally of a steel gray color on top, with the yellow subsoil and clay underneath, or what has become so well known as the best orange land of Florida. The climate, like that of all other high lands in South Florida, is perfectly healthy the year round, and many people who are abundantly able to choose their place of residence, live here summers and winters in preference to other countries. Many of the best people of Michigan, Ohio and Massachusetts, have been attracted to Altamonte by its favorable location for health and successful orange raising, and the thrift and intelligence of its inhabitants, who are almost entirely Northern people. Enough men of wealth and influence are already interested here to insure the future growth and success of the place, and the thousands of thrifty young trees, shrubs, plants, etc., of every variety that grows in Southern lands, will attest to the richness of its soil as well as the patience and energy of the few who came here ten or twelve years ago with nothing but their hands for capital, and who started the change that must in a few years make a blooming garden of what was then a silent wilderness. Hoosier and Shephard Springs have a wonderful attraction for the Northern visitor, and he exclaims, "Well! well!!" while they throw their crystal waters out and form a small lake so clear that one would say they were but a few inches in depth where they are many feet! The water as a bath, or taken inwardly, is very beneficial to patients troubled with rheumatism or any blood diseases, being strongly impregnated with sulphur and other minerals. Lake Brantley has a surface of about one square mile, and offers a splendid place for fishing, bathing, etc. The oldest orange groves at Altamonte have been set from ten to twelve years, but only two or three had been put out up to 1874 or 1875, and it was still three or four years later before people had enough faith in orange raising to go into it to any extent. Now there are new groves being started in all directions, while ten to fifteen thousand bearing trees bend beneath their heavy loads of fruit this year. Here can be seen seedling trees that have been set only nine or ten years, with from 1,000 to 1,500 oranges on each, and budded trees that have been out only four years, with from 200 to 500 oranges on each. Here are young groves that have cost considerably less than $1,000, that to-day would easily sell for $2,500, and still better, larger ones that have cost $3,000 or $4,000 that are now worth $10,000 to $15,000. Still this is no more than any grove will do in a good location, when cared for by a thorough and experienced man, and only goes to show that there is no investment in the world equal to a good orange grove.

The permanent inhabitants of Altamonte will number about 200, besides the great rush of Northern visitors who stay there only through the winter. The Michigan people are clustering around Hoosier Springs and Lake Brantley principally, while those from Massachusetts are interested near Snow's Station and Shephard Springs, and those from Ohio in still another direction. With all her natural attractions, and her wealthy and influential men, Altamonte may certainly look forward to a prosperous and brilliant future.

MAYO.

Four miles south of Longwood and fourteen from Sanford is Mayo Station, where are located several important industries, and about which in every direction are promising orange and lemon groves. The land is high and rolling pine, though just at the depot is a small patch of scrub which affords excellent and healthy building sites.

The first thing that attracts the attention is the large and well arranged saw and planing mill, with a capacity of 8,000 feet per day, owned and run by Messrs. Nevins & Prentis. About the mill yard are extensive piles of lumber ready for use. To the west is Lake Seminary, a pretty sheet of water, on which Dr. Nevins has a little steamer and several row boats. East of the track are several small and not specially attractive cabins, but as the primitive period is past they will doubtless soon give place to handsome and substantial buildings.

Just south of the saw mill is the ice factory of Dr. R. H. Nevins that has supplied this section and towns along the South Florida Railroad with ice for several years past. It originated from small beginnings, a little Pictet ice machine, with which the Dr. supplied his own household. Others wanted ice and the demand was so pressing that in 1880 he secured a machine with a daily capacity of 2,500 pounds. The demand greatly exceeding the supply, in 1881 he increased the capacity to 5,000 pounds. This however did not keep pace with the development of the country and the past summer the Doctor has built an immense new building a little farther south and put in an entirely new ice machine with all the latest improvements that will make twelve tons (24,000 pounds) of ice daily. It is frozen in large oblong blocks and is very firm, clear and pure, better even and more lasting than lake ice. With so largely increased capacity he will doubtless be able to supply a large scope of country.

Opposite the new ice factory, east of the railroad, Mr. J. A. Prentis has built a fine two story packing house where many thousands of the oranges and lemons raised in this vicinity will doubtless be assorted, wrapped, packed, branded and shipped for market. Just north of Mr. P's place is a small country store. To the east are occasional indications of piney woods and black jack and other oaks, though much has been cleared and the place supplied with numerous orange groves. Here, too, is the direct Maitland & Lake Jesup road, handsomely covered with saw dust. It runs directly through the homestead of

COL. RUDOLPH G. MAYO,

the pioneer settler of the place. He was born in Saxony, and came in 1849 to Virginia. In January, 1875, he came to Florida, and looking over a part of the State invested on the Hillsborough river, a few miles south of New Smyrna. Continuing his travels over a considerable part of the State, he settled on his present beautiful location, and commenced its improvement, it suiting him the best of any place he had seen. All about him were the piney woods interspersed with oak and a few unoccupied homesteaders' cabins, the homestead laws being enforced very loosely at that time.

The part of his land to the east of Nevins & Prentis he has laid out into lots 100 x 300 feet and sold a number. A few acres in the southeast corner fronting on a beautiful lake with part of his grove, he has just sold to Mr. A. F. Ackerman, of Staunton, Va. Between this and his home lot is a fine bay covered with heavy growth and filled with muck of so fine quality that it brings $3 a cord as a fertilizer.

The Col. has a very fine pine apple plantation of 13,500 plants, from which he derives a handsome income. On his residence lot are some 500 trees from three to ten years old, mostly budded. Besides these he has in grove 500 five years old trees, 200 three, 200 two, 6,000 nursery trees, three to five years old, and 30,000 one to two years old. The trees in grove are all budded and he has a number of the finest Mandarin orange trees we have seen, trees that bear remarkably large oranges, and one of very fine flavor ribbed fruit. He also has camphor trees, other trees in great variety, very fine lemons, variegated orange and lemon trees, etc.

His residence is on a handsome knoll overlooking a beautiful lake, with lovely shores and shady retreats. Around the house are a profusion of flowers and trailing vines. But the house itself is a beauty and unique, one of the very best contrived, finished and arranged in South Florida. To his genial and accomplished lady is given the credit of its conception.

DR. R. H. NEVINS

Has a lovely home to the west of Lake Seminary and northeast of Lakes Faith, Hope and Charity, pleasant bodies of water about a mile long. He has one of the largest and finest houses in South Florida, two stories in height, with broad piazzas, wide halls, high ceilings and attractive finish. It affords magnificent views in every direction. About the house are many flowers and the pillars and lattice work of the piazzas are covered with climbing jassamine and other vines. His fine bearing grove, stables, etc., are a few rods to the northwest. He has 700 trees of varied ages in grove, and some 4,000 nursery trees. The Doctor came here in 1879 from Waterford, Conn.

MR. J. A. PRENTIS,

Who came from New London, Conn., in November, 1881, has a fine thrifty grove of 1,400 trees, part bearing. Some are seedlings five to ten years old, and some budded from one to four years. Whoever has occasion to deal with any of the gentlemen mentioned will find them courteous, agreeable and straightforward in every respect.

THE QUINNIPIAC FERTILIZER COMPANY,

Of New London, Conn., is here represented by John A. Prentis. This Company have, the first year, put on the market the FISH BONE AND POTASH brand of their fertilizer, and the success attained has lead to the establishment at Mayo of a distributing warehouse for the further introduction of their goods.

MR. W. S. CHAPPELL,

Of New London, is engaged in the PACKING BUSINESS in connection with his business at the North, thus enabling the orange growers of this section to place their products without the trouble of packing, shipping and sending to markets which may be overstocked, and also saving all delay in returns. This is an enterprise which we have long required, and cannot fail of success.

MAITLAND.

One of the most beautiful, most healthful and most celebrated places in South Florida is Maitland, and many writers have been very enthusiastic in its praise, its thrifty orange groves and lovely scenery having a world wide reputation.

The South Florida railroad, which has so greatly aided in the development of the country, passes directly through the pretty village, which is fifteen miles south of Sanford and six north of Orlando, the county seat. Here are numerous pleasant residences surrounded by fruitful groves, and the yards are adorned with shrubbery, climbing vines, roses, etc., and the bloom of flowers may be seen during the entire year.

The lands are mostly high pine with here and there a piece of rich hammock or bay especially desirable for vegetable gardens. Beautiful clear water lakes delight the view from nearly every point and Lake Maitland is connected by a running stream with a chain of smaller lakes that will eventually be opened up for row and sail boats. The lakes are well stocked with fish.

Maitland is ninety feet above the St. Johns river and the climate is all that can be desired and very beneficial to weak and delicate constitutions. The place is also very free from insects and poisonous snakes. Society is excellent, people of means and culture from all parts of Union making their homes here, and there is as much freedom of thought and action as in any other part of the country.

Here are two first-class hotels, a number of boarding houses, Episcopal, Methodist and Roman Catholic churches, public and private schools, three good general merchandise stores, drug store, postoffice, telegraph office, town hall, livery stable, and near by a saw mill, ice factory, dairy farm, etc. In this center of a delightful region is

MR. R. T. PATTON'S REAL ESTATE AND LAND AGENCY.

Mr. P. has endeared himself to all the people of this section, and those who have had dealings with him, or the pleasure of his acquaintance, find him uniformly courteous, wide-awake and attentive to business and strictly reliable in all his statements and transactions.

He has scores of places on his books, both improved and unimproved, and one of the very finest teams in this section. He makes it his business to show the country to prospective buyers free of charge and being well posted on qualities of lands and their values present and prospective, he rarely fails to give the best of satisfaction to those seeking a delightful home or opportunities for profitable investment.

He has quite a number of places suited to men of moderate means that he is selling at remarkably low prices, many of them partially improved and with a few trees in bearing. Those seeking homes in this delightful country should not fail to see what genuine bargains he can offer before purchasing elsewhere.

The man of means who desires a healthful, lovely and profitable home should see some of the fine places on Mr. Patton's list. We would especially note one of fifty-one (51) acres on high rolling ground fronting on one of the most lovely lakes in this section. Here are 3,700 orange trees, 1,000 bearing and the others beginning to bear, 10,000 pine apple plants, in vigorous condition and fruiting heavily, very fine and choice specimens and varieties, bananas, guavas and numerous other fruits that thrive in this locality.

The residence is a very fine one, the buildings costing $13,000. About it are the varied kinds of shrubbery for which Orange county is noted and flowers in profusion. The views from the varied parts of the residence are lovely in the extreme and no locality can possibly be more healthful. It is also very near railroad, telegraph, churches, schools, stores and other concomitants of modern civilization.

A couple of other places that Mr. Patton has for sale are briefly described as follows:

Beautiful place on Lake Maitland, handsome new house, modern villa style, eight rooms, closets, store rooms, servants' quarters, etc., 15 acres of land fronting on lake. There are 375 orange trees, 200 bearing, rest to bear within a year, many budded with finest imported varieties. Forty bearing lemons and limes; 100 bearing guava bushes, 300 pineapples, and other small fruits. Place pays good percentage on value, and in all respects is one of the most desirable in Orange county. Price, $18,000.

Thirty-five acres adjoining above, all cleared and planted in orange trees, 1,100 budded with finest native and imported varieties; a number bearing and all to bear within two years if kept in their present thrifty condition. Fine garden spot fenced in and under cultivation. Beautiful building site on Lake Maitland, commanding a view of Lake Minnehaha. Price, $8,000.

Will sell both places for $25,000. The fifty acres making one of the handsomest estates in the county, near transportation, convenient to churches, etc., and in the midst of first-class society.

JUDGE W. H. M'BRAYER'S GROVE.

Conspicuous among the flourishing groves of Orange county is that of Judge W. H. McBrayer, an enterprising capitalist of Kentucky, who was attracted by the beauty of the country and the rich promises of the future. His orange grove lies along the margin of a trio of beautiful lakes, Faith, Hope and Charity, a half mile northwest of the prosperous village of Maitland. It contains 4,000 budded trees of uniform size, fresh and vigorous. Between Lakes Hope and Charity lies a picturesque island, densely shaded with oak and pine, a famous trysting place for the youth of the surrounding country, and a delightful resort for excursionists. On the opposing sides of the lakes the enterprising owner contemplates further and extensive improvements in the way of groves and buildings. A broad and well shaded avenue leads from the main road to this delightful spot, and tourists and travelers can easily find access and a hospitable welcome. The place is in care of Mr. S. F. Hicks, an experienced orange culturist, who attends to the interests of his principal during his absence.

WINTER PARK.

This delightful and attractive locality, destined to speedy development as the home of people of wealth culture and refinement, is situated on the South Florida railroad seventeen miles south of Sanford and four north of Orlando, on the beautiful Lake Osceola. One especially attractive feature here is

THE ROGERS HOUSE,

Pleasantly situated on the high shore of the lake, giving a delightful view. It is but a few rods from the Depot. The rooms are light, airy and reasonably commodious, the table is excellent and terms are reasonable. It is a delightful hostelry for the tourist, the business man or the winter visitor. Here one finds pure spring water, health giving air, fine opportunities for boating and fishing, etc. In brief no more pleasant resting place can be found in Florida and Mr. A. E. Rogers, the proprietor, and his excellent lady use every possible effort to make their guests stay agreeable, and they succeed.

OSCEOLA.

This lovely and peaceful locality, named from the friendly Indian chief who had his headquarters here, lies to the eastward of several of the most beautiful lakes in Florida. Its lands are excellent and it is surpassed in no respect. It is near the 28th degree of latitude and is one mile east of the Winter Park station on the South Florida Railroad. Here are numerous beautiful bearing groves, besides thousands of trees of the citrus family that will soon be laden with golden fruit.

The lakes are five in number: Osceola, Mizell, (named after the first living settler, Judge J. R. Mizell, who has the very best of lands and a fine bearing grove,) Berry, Virginia, and Maitland, and they are unsurpassed anywhere. It is in fact one of the choicest of locations in Florida.

MR. EDGAR RICHMOND

Has a very fine place at the east of this charming hamlet, with a fine two story house, commodious barns and a full supply of teams, agricultural tools, implements, etc. His land is principally high pine, but he has about twenty acres of choice hammock and bay lands, and a muck bed of about twenty acres of so fine quality that it sells for $3 per cord in situ, being a valuable fertilizer for pine lands.

He came here from Illinois in October, 1878, and took up a homestead. All was covered with the primeval forest characteristic of Florida. But intelligent and earnest effort works surprising changes and the woods have given place to cultivated fields and flourishing groves. He now has 500 thrifty, budded orange trees, 100 budded Sicily and Villa Frank lemon trees, some in bearing, besides guavas, bananas, pineapples, pomgranates, LeConte pears, grapes, ever bearing mulberries, etc. His yard is ornamented with very fine rose bushes, ivys, honeysuckle and other trailing vines, oleander, etc., a variety of shrubbery and flowers in abundance, his excellent and accomplished wife being a great lover of the beautiful and untiring in her efforts to make a lovely home, and she has met with wonderful success.

Besides ten acres in grove he has twenty acres in vegetables, and his lands are enclosed by substantial wire fences. Though his wife and himself and his two children have staid here winter and summer all these years, they have had no occasion for the services of a physician, and are naturally delighted with the country and have a place that could not be bought for $25,000.

JUDGE JOHN R. MIZELL.

The deputy U. S. Marshal, has one of the very finest tracts of 100 acres of lands in this section. This land is mostly the very best of the rolling, high pine lands of the State, and is a portion of a tract purchased by his father, David Mizell, in 1858, and where he brought up a large family long before the days of orange groves, securing a competency by general agriculture and stock raising, the land producing excellent cotton, sugar cane, corn, potatoes, peas, vegetables, etc., and being more free from frost than most localities.

Judge Mizell has a very pleasant residence surrounded by a variety of beautiful trees, shrubs and flowers in great abundance. He has a fine bearing grove of 500 thrifty orange and lemon trees and about 2,500 not yet come into bearing, and the number will increase annually. His residence overlooks four beautiful lakes and he has, without exaggeration, one of the finest locations in Florida, as well as one of the most healthful, his four children never having required the services of a physician though the eldest is fourteen. This fine place could not be purchased for less than $30,000.

MR. WILSON PHELPS,.

A native of New York, came to Osceola, Oct. 20th, 1874, from Illinois and located a homestead, afterwards purchasing more land. The following winter he cleared land and set out nearly 1,100 trees in grove form, besides a nursery of 1,000 trees, and planted orange seed from which he raised over 10,000 trees. Since then he has added to his groves from year to year and there are now in grove 3,600 trees that he set out, a portion of which he has sold. He has all the leading and popular varieties of fruit most prized for eating and transportation : oranges, limes, lemons, guavas, pine apples, Le-Conte pears, Surinam cherries, Japan persimmons, Scuppernong grapes and other varieties too numerous to mention. Mr. Phelps has an elegant two story residence and as fine grounds as are likely to be found in South Florida. His location is also most excellent and affords a lovely view of land and water. He came for the benefit of his health and has found what he sought as well as material prosperity.

MR. H. H. BERRY,

A veritable pioneer, came from Tallahassee and located a homestead in 1872, giving it such attention as the law at that time required. A few years since he moved here with his family and gave his whole attention to his place, wagon making and general blacksmithing, employing several men. He has just removed his shop to Orlando. He has a fine grove of 300 trees, partly bearing, set out in 1874, and 225 set two years since. Being one of the first settlers, as a natural consequence he has very fine land, a selection of the best. As a matter of course his excellent wife has the house surrounded by a profusion of flowers, etc.

MR. A. E. ROGERS,

Until recently the village store keeper, has a pretty place with 400 trees, about 100 of which are nine to ten years old, and part bearing. The balance are two and three years old.

Mr. Comstock has a very fine place, cared for by Mr. Wilson Phelps; Messrs. E. K. Pierce, B. L. Clark and R. H. Thayer from Massachusetts, have very pretty places with young groves, and Mr. Livingston, the postmaster, has a pleasant place. There are several other improved places.

FORMOSA.

This charming locality is situate immediately north of and adjacent to Wilcox, but separated from Wilcox by the creek which connects Lakes Ivanhoe and Formosa. This is Howell creek, which passing through Lakes Rowena, Sue, Virginia, Mizell, Osceola, Maitland and Howell, empties into Lake Jesup between Tuscawilla and Clifton Springs. By dredging and locks steamboat communication can be had with Lake Jesup, thence *ad infinitum*. Mr. Burleigh's saw, planing, lath and shingle mills, Gov. Sinclair's cotton gins, grist mill and starch factory, are its manufacturing interests. Beautiful lakes—Ivanhoe, Formosa, Rowena, Sue and Estell. Here are the splendid groves of Messrs. Wheeler, Sinclair, Prof. Logan, Allen, Kollock, Doyle, Sanxay, Shattucks and Jacocks; some are bearing, the others well established and thrifty, all made without the aid of commercial fertilizer to any great extent, and notably Jacocks' grove, which has been brought to bearing solely by dint of direct study of the *how* to grow an orange tree without such aid. Jacocks may be classed the pioneer and began without means, his only capital being determination to succeed. Then it required nerve, because of distance from public transportation, the sparcity of settlers and impecunious circumstances of some. Being a judge of good land, a studious operator at the hoe, plow and ax, and adroit in judicious pruning and budding, he is almost in the enjoyment of the end determined on. Others recognizing his skill and superior training in the culture of the orange and other fruits, gave him superintendency of their interests, and he has in charge several groves that he resurrected and now has them far advanced. He makes *grove* culture a specialty, and is always watchful of his patrons' interests, advancing their interests by strict application and a knowledge of what is needed. Parties just beginning to set groves, and non-residents notably, would save money by securing the services of Mr. Jacocks, giving him *carte blanche* commission. Faithful, true and tried, he is an arboriculturist of true merit.

WILLCOX.
GROVE OF DR. GEORGE F. SHATTUCK.

Do you desire a lovely view, one of the most lovely in South Florida, amid delightful surroundings, where every prospect pleases and the very atmosphere is instinct with health and buoyant life? Then take your stand on the spot where Dr. Shattuck, an eminent physician, whose office is at 1232 S. Tenth St., Philadelphia, Pa., proposes to locate his winter home. His lot of 21½ acres is bounded on the north by Lake Estell, east by Lake Rowena, and south by Lake Formosa—all lovely lakes. To the west is the beautiful plat of 25 acres of J. P. Sanxay, Esq., of Brooklyn, N. Y., of whom Dr. S. purchased his tract the first of last January, through Sinclair's enterprising and reliable land agency of Orlando, the firm mentioned being Hon. J. G. Sinclair and N. L. Mills, Esq., gentlemen with whom it is a pleasure to deal.

Yet west comes the lot of C. W. Jacocks, Esq., the treasurer of Orange county, with his fine residence and attractive grove. North and west is Mr. M. J. Doyle's fine bearing grove of six acres. Beautiful lakes and choice groves meet the eye on every hand, and the South Florida railroad passes through on the west; also the county road. So delighted was the Doctor with his investment of $2,450 for this choice section that he immediately made a New Year's present of it to his wife, and consigned it to the conscientious care of C. W. Jacocks, Esq., with instructions to make the best possible grove, using the very best quality of everything needful, and that too without stint. Everybody knows that Jacocks knows how to make a grove, and also whether it be trees, fertilizers or labor he will have none but the best.

He has already set out some twelve acres, some 600 orange, 500 lemon and 100 lime trees. Also a few peach, LeConte pear and fig trees, and soon expects to have out olives, citron, Japan persimmon, grapes, bananas, pineapples, guavas, English walnuts, almond and pecan trees, and in fact as large a variety of growths as give any promise of being adapted to the soil and climate.

Dr. Shattuck, a physician and surgeon of large practice, has traveled quite extensively North, South, East and West, and knowing whereof he speaks, is very enthusiastic regarding Orange county and says that that part of Florida of which it is the center is a great Sanitarium, and that thousands of the Northern people would prolong their lives five, ten, and even twenty or more years if they would reside in Orange county from the first of November to the first of May of each year, and that thousands would gladly enjoy their time and money in this favored section if they were aware of a half the benefits and advantages they could thus secure. He says that take it all in all for good health and a pleasant place to live in there is no State equal to Florida, and that Orange county is for health the best part of the State.

MR. M. CONWAY'S GROVE.

To see a beautiful orange and lemon grove is a delight to the eye and to all the higher senses. To see and to eat of the golden fruit in its native lusciousness gives an increased feeling of sympathy for Mother Eve, and causes us to no longer wonder that she listened to the serpent and Adam to his Eve, for these golden apples of the Hesperides are the forbidden fruit of the Jews. Thus we mused as a few days since we visited the pleasant and thriving grove of M. Conway, Esq., two miles northerly from his well stocked general merchandise store at Wilcox.

Mr. C. came here from Savannah, Ga., where he had had a life long experience in the hotel business, in 1873, and took up a homestead. He returned in 1875 and has since resided here. He was seriously troubled with rheumatism but this disappeared. His homestead is fertile, rolling high pine land on the east shore of the beautiful Lake Killarney. He at first set out 400 trees, oranges, lemons, limes, etc., and has since added 800. Of these 100 bloomed this year, and he expects at least 600 next year. The grove has had but little attention and no fertilization until the past four years.

but it is now in excellent condition and well cultivated. The fruit is of the choicest varieties. He also gives considerable attention to the cultivation of vegetables and they are in a very promising condition.

TAVARES.
THE GREAT RAILROAD CENTER OF SOUTH FLORIDA.

The youngest of all the towns of Orange county, Tavares is now the fourth in point of population while in present and growing importance it ranks first.

Tavares is located on a peninsula, bounded on the north by Lake Eustis, on the south by Lake Dora and on the west by the Oclawaha river. The land around Tavares is high, rolling and beautiful, and consists of hammock and pine lands. Here can be seen the bearing grove belonging to the Peninsular Land, Transportation and Manufacturing Company, containing some of the largest trees in the county.

Tavares, as a center of transportation, has no equal in South Florida. In season of high water it is connected with the St. Johns river by steamboat transportation through the Oclawaha river. The St. Johns & Lake Eustis Railroad is now completed into the town and the Company has just constructed a commodious warehouse and wharf for their lake business. The Transit and Peninsular Railroad, which connects with the entire railroad system of the United States, is now laying iron to Leesburg, and will be finished into Tavares the present winter. The Tavares, Orlando & Atlantic Railroad is now building from Tavares taward Orlando, and a syndicate has been formed to build the Tavares & Lake Monroe Railroad. These four lines of transportation are now actually building. In addition, the Florida Southern and the International will almost certainly extend their lines to this place so as to share in the lake business, which grows of greater importance every month.

Tavares is now the commercial and traveling entreport for the entire section of country contiguous to Lakes Dora, Beauclair, Carleton, Ola and Apopka. It supplies the settlements and villages of Mount Dora, Tangerine, Sorrento, Zellwood, Carleton, West Apopka, Oakland, Starke Lake, Minneola and other points, and will, within the next three years, be the greatest shipping point in all this region of Florida.

Situated between two large lakes Tavares is unusually well protected from frosts and is widely known for this immunity from danger. Here may be seen guava trees over ten years of age. For healthfulness it has no superior in the State, and it has the best water for drinking purposes in this entire section.

As a point for successful business enterprises, Tavares offers inducements far exceeding any other place in South Florida. At present there are but two stores there, but now that the railroad is operating to this point, and the steamboat service to the lakes is begun, a business of half a million dollars per annum awaits all who embark. A wholesale grocery store, a builders' hardware store and other mercantile ventures will pay heavy profits.

The lands around Tavares are peculiarly adapted to the cultivation of vegetables, and the closeness to transportation gives growers an advantage not to be found elsewhere.

Town lots, villa sites, orange grove lands, can be obtained at moderate prices on advantageous terms. Building lots and lumber will be GIVEN to persons engaging in manufacturing enterprises.

Tavares is reached from Jacksonville by the St. Johns river steamers to Astor, thence by rail on the St. Johns & Lake Eustis railroad. As soon as the Transit and Peninsular railroad is completed, there will be an all rail route with any part of the United States.

As a winter resort Tavares is one of the most inviting in South Florida. The hunting and fishing are unequalled. Here is the "Peninsular Hotel," the best hotel in the Lake Region. The Mitchell House, now approaching completion, will be open in December for the accommodation of the traveling public.

Persons desiring further information will address the Peninsular Land, Transportation and Manufacturing Company, Tavares, Orange county, Florida.

ALEX. ST. CLAIR-ABRAMS, Pres't.

WM. H. LATIMER. Sec'y and Treas.

EUSTIS.

A LIVE MAN.

John A. Macdonald of Eustis, Orange county, Florida, has done so much for the development of South Florida and Orange county in particular, that a description of the county and no mention of him would be like the play of Hamlet and Hamlet left out. With a reputation, National in its extent, for honesty, ability and promptness, he finds the calls upon him for information and services so vast and wide spread that he has been compelled to publish a new book, "PLAIN TALK ABOUT FLORIDA," mailed free for 25 cents, together with his map of Eustis. The Lake Region, embraces most of Orange and part of Sumter and some of Polk county. Besides the immense business in private lands, he has a constantly increasing corps of correspondents who are calling on him to select Government lands for them. He can procure you 40 acres of choice Orange land for $60. He has devoted seventeen years to the development of the United States lands in the State. He knows the whole region better than any other man living; has settled more than two thousand families on prosperous and happy homes. United States land selected by him four years ago is now worth from $25 to $400 per acre; land selected two years ago is now worth $10 to $50 per acre—cost $1.25. He is now selecting Government land equally as good, that in three to five years will be worth $100 per acre—40 acres costs $60. If you want a beautiful tract of improved or unimproved land in Orange, Sumter, Polk, Hernando, Hillsborough, or adjoining counties, for a home or investment, write him and all questions will be truthfully answered. He refers to any of his settlers and to leading citizens in every State and Territory of the Union and in Canada. Sixty dollars invested now will be a home and a fortune in a few years.

CHAS. T. SMITH & CO.,

General merchants, Fort Mason and Eustis, Orange county, Florida, have the largest and best assorted stocks to be found in the Lake Region. Supplies for fruit and vegetable growers always on hand. Cotton seed meal, Forrester and Bradley fertilizers, corn, hay, flour. etc., kept in large quantities. A general stock of house furnishing goods, bed room suits, spring bedding, etc. Domestic and New Home Sewing Machines also kept in stock. Also a full line of metalic burial cases, wood caskets and coffins.

T. T. Jackson is in charge of the Eustis house.

DUNCAN'S BAAZAR.

Ice cream saloon, ice lemonade, soda water, fruit, cigars, confectionery, oysters.

SAMUEL W. DUNCAN has recently opened the above establishment. Being an experienced artist in the art of compounding the various cooling draughts and delicacies of such an establishment, he has already won an enviable reputation.

No swill, no slops; everything clean, neat and inviting. He will make a specialty of oysters in their season, and raw, fried or stewed, you can get them. Choice apples will be a specialty. Orders from a distance for oranges, lemons, limes and guavas promptly attended to.

THE SEMI-TROPICAL.

This wide awake and ably edited newspaper which is thoroughly devoted to, and pre-eminently representative of the interests of the "Great Lake Region," of Orange county, Florida, in particular, and of South Florida in general, is published every Saturday at the rapidly growing town of Eustis, situated on a lovely lake of the same name, which hopes to be the metropolis of that section. It gives reliable information on the climate, soil, productions and resources of Orange county. Also weather reports, statistics and general information, showing the facts in regard to all parts of the remarkable section of country known as South Florida, the home of the orange and many other delicious semi-tropical fruits.

Being particularly devoted to the interests and development of the lovely section of country known as the "Great Lake Region," it is a very valuable paper for the fruit or vegetable grower, the property holder, business man or prospector, and also for the home circle. All can get desirable information from its pages. Terms, $1.50 per year in advance. Send for specimen copy to Geo. F. Miner, editor and publisher, Eustis, Fla.

THE FLORIDA AGRICULTURAL COMPANY, LIMITED, OF LONDON, ENGLAND.

The lands owned by this company comprise about 40,000 acres, situated on Lake East Tahopekaliga. The lake affords a northeast water protection of six miles, and besides these substantial advantages offers natural attractions which are inseparable from so beautiful a sheet of water.

The dredge boat of the Land and Improvement Company is now engaged and is making rapid progress in cutting the canal between Lake Tahopekaliga and East Tahopekaliga and direct water communication will thus be obtained between the Company's lands and Kissimmee City.

The lands are of every quality, embracing large tracts of saw grass of unsurpassed fertility for the cultivation of sugar which it is confidently believed will be drained on the completion of the canal.

The general appearance of the high lands is rolling and attractive, the situation and the soil offering every advantage for the cultivation of the orange and the whole citrus family. Patches of high hammock are scattered throughout the property, well adapted for truck farming and otherwise. These lands this Company propose to settle by colonization both from the United States and England, and the solid inducements and advantages offered cannot fail to attract the attention of residents in those less favored districts.

The general plan is to offer to visitors small farms ready fenced and cleared with house which can be built to suit the taste of the purchaser; also groves ready planted with orange or other trees of any age which the purchaser may desire.

The Company's model farms and groves are made on a uniform plan and offered at reduced rates. A town has been laid out and lots are reserved for churches, schools and public recreation grounds. A good saw mill is on the ground and a stock of 250,000 feet of lumber on hand which is reserved for the use of settlers and will be offered to them at prices lower than the lowest.

As soon as the canal is completed the company will run a steam boat between the estate and Kissimmee, and will offer to settlers the transportation of their goods and farm products at greatly reduced prices, and especial accommodations will be extended to settlers during the first year of residence.

The Company will guarantee to employ bona fide settlers in preference to all others, as long as the former shall give satisfaction.

The Company is erecting stores and boarding houses, planting orange nurseries and carrying out all these works with the view of providing settlers with provisions and materials at the minimum of cost, so that the immigrants may be certain of obtaining a large supply of everything they can desire at prices which could hardly be realized by individuals.

Special arrangements will be made to meet the desire and convenience of any purchaser, and the officers of the Company will make it their endeavor to study the different ideas and wishes of all so that if the above does not coincide with the views of any intending visitor, fuller information can be obtained by applying by letter or personally to

Mr. E. N. Fell, Gen. Man'r.
Kissimmee City, Fla.

LIVINGSTON & WALLACE, REAL ESTATE AGENTS,

Orlando, Florida. Buy and sell orange groves and orange lands in Orange county, and examine deeds.

Mr. J. H. Livingston, the senior of the above firm, is from the old State of Kentucky, where he resided in the capacity of tiller of the soil and stock raiser on the Blue Grass of that State, until he came farther south.

The past seven years he has spent in the county of Orange from choice, that choice being made after an extended prospecting tour of South Florida, embracing all the lands contiguous to and on the Atlantic and Gulf coasts. For some years his energies were concentrated in making two orange groves, one of which he sold last year for $10,000 cash, the other his family now enjoy the fruits of, together with various other groves and tracts well located in Orange county.

His family and himself have enjoyed perfect health all these years, having yet to employ the first M. D. in the family. Of such facts many instances can be enumerated.

The health of Orange county is beyond question, proper location having much to do with it. Of this, and the soils adapted to the successful growth of the orange, Mr. Livingston's long experience is worth much. In this particular he takes great pains with all buyers, to see that they get what they desire, and as an agent, does all in his power that experience has taught him to aid all buyers in these very important particulars.

The same may be said of Mr. J. L. Wallace, the junior partner, with the exception that Mr. Wallace has not had quite as long an experience. Mr. Wallace came here three years ago from the West, where he had been a commercial traveler in Illinois, Iowa and Nebraska for a number of years, enjoying the confidence of a large circle of friends. His history here has been the same, and like the senior he enjoys the confidence of all the old citizens of Orange county.

As Land Agents, these gentlemen have on their books valuable groves in bearing, as well as younger groves and wild lands aggregating thousands of acres. These groves and lands are near Orlando, Maitland, Winter Park, South Apopka, and that beautiful lake country four miles east of the railroad at Maitland, known as the Howell and the Woronoco Lake region. These lands are known for their health and adaptability for oranges, lemons, limes, guavas, pineapples, etc. etc., as also for vegetables of all kinds.

They solicit correspondence, and any information desired will be promptly given. Fine carriages in readiness.

SINCLAIR'S REAL ESTATE AGENCY,
AT ORLANDO.

There is no agency in the county whose success has been so marked as this. From a small beginning in April, 1881, a course of square dealing has built up a business second to none of the kind in the State.

Hon. John G. Sinclair, the senior member of this firm, came here from New Hampshire in November, 1879, for the purpose of engaging in the manufacture of starch from the Cassava root, having been a large manufacturer at the North. Having a very extensive acquaintance in New England, he had occasion to purchase many places for his friends North, and parties here, seeing his opportunities, applied to him to sell for them. Applications from both buyers and sellers became so numerous that in April, 1881, he took out his first license. From that date to July, 1882, a period of fourteen months, although for a considerable time he had established no office and had no assistant, his sales aggregated $131,187. At that time it became apparent that the business had reached a magnitude that rendered it impossible for him to carry it along alone, and he employed Mr. N. L. Mills, of Burlington, Iowa, as assistant, who developed such capacity for the business that in November of the same year he was admitted as a partner.

From July 1, 1882, to Sept. 1, 1883, again fourteen months, their sales aggregated more than $275,000, more than doubling that of the first fourteen months, and the sales of September and October of the present year have amounted to more than three times those of the corresponding months of last year. These sales have been made to parties from nearly every State in the Union, in many instances to those who had never met either member of the firm, but who left it entirely to their discretion to select lands for them. It is the boast of this agency, and we believe it to be well founded, that there is no party to whom they have sold who charge them with any misrepresentation, and that there is no single piece of property sold by them prior to September 1, 1883, which will not sell for an advance on the price then paid. This is a remarkable statement when the liability of new settlers to change their mind or to become homesick is considered, but we know of many instances among their early sales where property has quadrupled in value. It is a pleasure to us to bear witness to the probity and success of this agency on account of its manly and honorable treatment of ourself a couple of years since, when we came from Massachusetts with little expectation of continued life, having been compelled to sacrifice a flourishing newspaper and job printing business because of increasing ill health, the leading physicians informing us that our only possible hope was in the genial climate of Florida, where we might possibly triumph over the catarrh, rheumatism and malaria that had brought us to the crumbling brink of the grave.

Through Sinclair's agency we found a piece of land that we thought would suit us for a home and put up a handsome sum as part payment, Mr. Sinclair having the deeds made out. But before completing the purchase we found a handsome tract of Government land at Lake Woronoco and entered a homestead. Upon stating the facts to the gentlemen of the agency, they not only released us from our agreement but refunded every dollar of the money we had advanced, though they could legally have kept every dollar.

It is by similiar acts of kindness and a course of fair dealing that this agency has laid its solid foundations and thus early established an attractive reputation throughout the county and it is now receiving its reward in a splendid business.

Every piece of property placed upon the books of this agency is thoroughly inspected by one of its members or a competent assistant. Titles are carefully examined and full abstracts of titles from the county records certified by the clerk of the Circuit Court are furnished free to purchasers. So thoroughly has this been done that in but a single instance has a title been questioned, and in that case the decision of the court sustained the title obtained through this agency.

Their office is on the corner of Orange and Pine streets, opposite the Charleston and Magnolia Hotels, and is the headquarters for newcomers. Fine specimens of fruits and products of Florida are kept there on exhibition. Printed matter relating to Florida, local papers, etc., are constantly kept for gratuitous circulation. Town, county and State maps for reference hang upon the walls, and information on all points interesting to proposed immigrants is cheerfully given. Good horses with comfortable covered carriages are in their shed and stable near the office, with careful drivers constantly in waiting to convey strangers, free of charge, to any points of interest in and about town and to any property offered by the agency for sale, and an efficient clerk is employed to answer all letters of inquiry under the supervision of the proprietors, both of whom show their faith in Florida by their works, Mr Sinclair having put out two groves of 800 trees each, one on the place at Wilcox on which he resides, (called Interlaken in Barbour's Book on Florida) beautifully situated on Lakes Ivanhoe and Formosa, the other on Hammock land on Lake Rowena, both of which groves are as fine of their age as any in this vicinity, and are well worthy of examination. Mr. Mills has bought ten acres in a fine location within the corporate limits of Orlando, on what is known as Whilldin's addition, and is to build and put out a grove on a part of it, selling the balance for building lots. This agency has probably nine-tenths of the properties for sale in and around Orlando exclusively on its books. Also some of the best at Maitland, Longwood and Apopka, some thousands of acres between Lakes Apopka and Butler, and large tracts along the line of the South Florida Railroad in Polk county, selected by an experienced surveyor. We cheerfully commend this enterprising firm to our readers.

BIDDELL & CRUMPLER,
500,000 ACRES OF GOVERNMENT LANDS.

This firm, G. W. Biddell and M. O. Crumpler, have State, Disston and Railroad lands from which to make selections. We have spared no time or money in obtaining knowledge as to the whereabouts and quality of the above vacant lands. These lands consist of Hammock, (high and low), Pine, (rolling and table), and prairie, admirably adapted to oranges, corn, sugar cane, rice, and vegetables. In fact everything usually grown in South Florida. For further information, address us with 2 cent stamp to cover postage. All letters promptly answered, free of charge. Correspondence solicited. Address at Orlando, Orange county, Florida.

The above gentlemen are in the real estate business in the manner shown in their advertisement, in order to accommodate not only men of large means, but those who may desire a home in Florida, having but little to invest. They are both men of large experience, having been so engaged in various other States. The senior as well as the junior of the firm have selected these lands from a personal search through the several counties mentioned, with the view to meet the wants of every one, not only as to value in money, but as to their adaptation to the orange and all semi-tropical fruits and vegetables, this latter soon to become one of the best paying industries in Florida.

They have under their supervision and on their books for sale, vacant lands in South Florida, embracing Government, State, Disston, Internal-Improvement, Seminary, school proper, school indemnity, and Railroad lands, of which they have full and complete maps got up for them by the best engineers at large expense. With these descriptive maps they can show the relative position of thousands of acres, enabling the purchaser to decide at their office the points of observation.

These lands are located in Orange, Sumter, Polk, Hillsborough, Hernando and Manatee counties. From this vast body they have been the means of selling many thousand acres during the past year. In fact they have few idle moments, so pushed are they with applications and purchasers. Their prices are moderate, making lands within reach of all. They are offering from 40 acres up to thousands in a body.

All business intrusted to them will receive prompt attention and all moneys be properly accounted for. Parties can do as well by sending their orders as to come in person. They make all selections as nearly according to written instructions as is possible, and by so doing they meet the wants of every one, and all are satisfied. This has proven the case in numerous instances this past summer, and will more than double in ratio this season. They have some large bodies of wild lands located years ago by competent men, when the country was in its wilds, and only a settler here and there, hence giving them the choice of the country. Prices of land vary according to location and their adaptation to use for oranges, vegetables, etc., nearness to railroads and towns, lakes and other advantages. They have many thousand acres of the most valuable lands in South Florida, at from $2.50 to $25.00 per acre.

MR. O. W. PRINCE.

What an enterprising and industrious man can do in Florida, is well illustrated by the experience and success of Mr. O. W. Prince, one of the leading merchants in Orlando. He moved to Orange county with his father in 1869, worked for him two years and at the age of 19 years started for himself, working for small wages. In 1874 he secured a homestead near Lake Apopka and commenced improving it and setting out a grove, to which he devoted all the means he could spare, which was but little, as he had married and had a family to support from his earnings.

The trees he set were very young and small, and since that time he has added to his grove from year to year until now he has 800 trees—oranges, lemons and limes—in very fine and thrifty condition, some 300 large enough to bear and 100 laden with fruit in his grove of fourteen acres, which would readily bring $10,000. It is situated a mile and a half northwest of Apopka City on the line of the Tavares, Orlando & Atlantic Railroad, which passes through his homestead. He has hired all his work done since commencing his grove.

In 1880 he moved to Orlando and commenced business on his own account with a capital of $700, Mr. S. A. Luckey, one of the prosperous pioneers of this section building him a store just south of the present Charleston Hotel, (formerly the Luckey House). Last year he built himself a fine store house and dwelling, with sixty feet front on Orange street, and opposite his former place of business, for which he has since been offered $4,000 in cash. Every available spot in the yard to the rear is filled with a nursery of thrifty and vigorous fruit trees.

He now has a very finely stocked general merchandise store, carrying some $6,000 to $10,000 worth of goods, comprising dry goods, notions, clothing, gents' furnishing goods, hats, caps, shoes, and all kinds of family and fancy groceries and provisions, which he sells as cheap as any house in town. He buys most of his groceries from the celebrated house of H. K. & F. B. Thurber & Co., of New York City, and prides himself on having goods of the very best quality in every department.

From this instance can be seen what little money with untiring energy and determination will do in Orange county, especially when coupled with sterling rectitude and integrity as in the case of Mr. Prince, who is universally esteemed for his honorable and straightforward dealing, and whose word is as good as his bond.

MR. JOHN A. WORTHEN,

A CIVIL ENGINEER, ARCHITECT AND SURVEYOR, a native of Vermont and graduate of Dartsmouth College, N. H., has purchased property and located at Orlando. He has been employed for several years in the line of his profession on the railroads of the Northwestern territories, and for the past two years in the service of the General Government as civil engineer, improving the navigation of the Mississippi. He comes highly recommended and is an unquestionably capable man well deserving the confidence and patronage of the community, and is ready to attend to any of their wants in his line of business.

T. J. ADAMS, LANDS ENTERED AND FOR SALE.

T. J. Adams, formerly of Chicago, Illinois, for eight years past a resident of Orange county, Florida, engaged in orange growing.

Improved and unimproved lands for sale in different parts of the county. Improved places from $1,000 to $12,000. Unimproved lands from $5 to $150 per acre. These lands were selected at an early day and include some of the best in the county.

Has examined the vacant lands throughout the county, and can make desirable selections. Is a good judge of the different Florida soils and never enters *swamps, lakes or scrub* for orange groves.

State and United States land $1.25 per acre.

Letters of inquiry promptly replied to. Address,
T. J. ADAMS,
P. O. Box 165. Orlando, Fla.

MARK R. BACON, ABSTRACTS OF LAND TITLES.

Mark R. Bacon, Orlando, Orange county, Florida, (formerly law partner of Hon. James McCartney, the present attorney general of Illinois). Examines land titles, gives opinions, pays taxes, selects, locates, and enters Government and State lands. Began and completed the only set of Abstract books of Land Titles in Orange county, therefore has a better knowledge of the titles to the lands in this county than any other person. Has personally inspected the lands in every part of the county and most of the State. Has land of his own in every part of the county for sale at from $5 per acre up.

U. S. Government land $1.25 per acre.

☞ Also land, improved and unimproved, in several different counties in Illinois to sell, or will trade for Florida lands.

Address at Orlando, Orange county, or Ocala, Marion county, Florida.

ORLANDO LABOR EXCHANGE.

Situations procured for reliable farm, mechanical and domestic laborers. Address, with stamp,
LABOR EXCHANGE,
Orlando, Fla.

TWO MODEL GROVES.

The two groves of Hon. Lewis Lawrence, of Utica, N. Y., one situated at Maitland and one near Winter Park, are models of neatness and marvels of rapid growth. This is due to the methods employed by Mr. Lawrence in their culture, and to the care he has bestowed upon his trees. That others may profit by his experience and successes, we give a general outline of his manner of treating his trees.

The grove at Maitland, of six and a half acres, was set out by Mr. L. in 1876. For two years the care of the trees was not very thorough, and they made but an indifferent growth. At the end of that time Mr. L. decided to force them. He therefore prepared a compost of muck, potash, lime and Stockbridge fertilizer, and applied thirty-six cords of this broadcast to the grove. This gave the trees a vigorous start. Since then, becoming convinced of the superior value of Forrester's fertilizers, he has used it exclusively, giving a broadcast dressing of 500 pounds per acre twice a year. His trees have made a marvelous growth, being now the delight of his heart, and receiving the attention and favorable comment of every one who sees them.

Early in the summer of 1881, Mr. L. purchased a tract comprising twenty-five acres of land and fifteen of water on the south side of Lake Maitland, near Winter Park. This he had thoroughly cleared, grubbed and burned, making it as clean as a garden. In the November following he set out 2,400 budded trees obtained from the Belair grove. They are set in hexagonal form, about 100 to the acre. At transplanting he gave them one pound of Forrester's fertilizer to the tree, and followed this a few weeks later with a broadcast dressing of 500 pounds to the acre. He has followed out this system of semi-annual dressings of 500 pounds of Forrester per acre since then with the most satisfactory results. He allows grass to grow among his trees until the ground is well covered, when he cuts it with machines and plows it under, thus adding vegetable matter as well. Several of his small trees, only set two years ago, have borne fruit the present season. Thorough tillage and liberal fertilization have accomplished all this and no man in Orange county can show more healthy or rapidly growing trees.

During the present season he has put in a caloric pump, large water tank, and system of underground pipes so that he can, in a dry season, thoroughly irrigate this young grove. He is systematic, methodical and thorough in everything, and does well whatever he undertakes. His success will stimulate and his methods instruct others.

C. A. BOONE & CO.,
SUCCESSORS TO PATRICK & BOONE.

Dealers in all kinds of hardware and furnishing goods. The largest and best assorted stock of crockery and glassware, China, tin, wood and willow ware and hollow ware, wall paper and curtain fixtures. Sewing machines, New Home, Houshold and American. We have a complete stock of furniture, spring beds, mattresses, matting, pillows, wardrobes, desks, stoves, etc. We are headquarters for everything in this line, and we guarantee our Iron King to cook better and last longer than any cook stove made.

We handle the largest assortment and best stock of paints, oils, varnishes, colors, whiting, brushes, etc., kept in the country. Also the best brands of table and pocket cutlery and carpenter's tools to be had anywhere, direct from the hands of the manufacturers.

Buggy and wagon harness, saddles, bridles, plowmen's outfits.

The largest and completest stock of agricultural implements, such as plows, hoes, spades, rakes, shovels, axes, mattocks, grub hoes, harrows, guns, hunting outfits, amunition, fishing tackle, base balls and bats.

We make specialties of the following: Barbed wire, drive wells, rubber and leather belting. Also sole agents for the celebrated Cotton Gaudy Belting, the best in use.

Orange boxes and wraps in large quantities during the season. Doors, sash and blinds at Jacksonville prices. We guarantee you better goods for the price and lower prices for the goods than you will find anywhere in South Florida.

C. A. BOONE & CO.

THE OLD RELIABLE STORE,
W. G. WHITE, ORLANDO, FLA.

Established 1878; 110x40 feet, two stories and barn. Chuck full of A No. 1 guaranteed supplies of all kinds. Everything a newcomer needs. Our stock is unrivaled; styles unequaled; quantity unsurpassed.; prices below competition. Call on us to buy your supplies for self, house, farm, grove and stock. Polite clerks, with determined efforts, will please you. Respectfully,

W. G. WHITE.

CLIFTON SPRINGS, ON LAKE JESUP,
ORANGE COUNTY, FLORIDA.

The famous pic-nic resort for all Sanford, Tuskawilla, Lake Charm and all surrounding country, is one of the most charmingly beautiful situations in all Florida. It is on the south side of Lake Jesup, which is a magnificent expanse of water, seventeen miles long and five miles wide. Clifton Springs takes its name from Dr. Henry Foster's place in Western, N. Y., and from the great number and variety of Sulphur Springs all in a short distance of each other. The location is a beautiful one: luxuriant tropical growth. The shore is a hard, white sand beach, and rises up from the water's edge to a height of ten feet. It presents a most eligible hotel site, is in the center of a magnificent belt of orange land, thickly studded with orange groves. The waters are full of fine fish and the hammocks are alive with game of all kinds. It is rapidly growing into notice, and will, in a short while, become a great winter resort. It is the property of Mr. W. G. White, the merchant of Orlando, Florida, who wishes to sell a part of it for a hotel, which, if properly managed, will prove a grand success.

DR. R. H. McFARLAND'S RESIDENCE.

At the south of a chain of beautiful lakes that spread out northward like a meandering river, and about a mile and a quarter southerly from Orlando, is the pleasant residence of Dr. McFarland, embowered amid a profusion of flowers and with a carpet of Bermuda grass that extends down the hill to the Lake Lancaster. Born in Pennsylvania he was for many years a resident of Kentucky from whence he came here Nov. 24, 1875, and bought a fine place of 60 acres. He was educated as an allopathic physician, which mode of treatment he practiced for twelve years, but for the past 30 years has been one of the most successful of Homeopathic physicians. He has a fine grove of 800 orange trees, 100 lemon, 25 Tahiti lime, 10 Japan plums, an acre of guavas, large quantity of Catalina guavas, Honey and Peen-to peaches, wild goose plum, Japan persimmon, LeConte pears, raspberries, blackberries, strawberries, pineapples, bananas, Concord and Delaware grapes, pawpaw, pecan, Surinam cherries, tea plants, white and Russian mulberries, etc., etc. On his place of 40 acres, named "The Oaks," he also has 400 orange, 200 guava and 50 lemon trees, besides limes, tea plant, etc. In fact pages might be filled with a description of this lovely place, his excellent wife's success with flowers, and the many charms and advantages both natural and artificial.

MR. S. A. LUCKEY.

As an illustration of what may be accomplished by pluck, intelligent energy and honorable dealing, we cite the case of Mr. S. A. Lucky, who has a fine place of about 500 acres some two miles east of Orlando, besides lands in other sections. He reached here from Georgia, Christmas day, 1870, with little means and a large family, rented lands and lived in a tent. His first attempts, by unexpected losses, used up what little means he had, and at the end of the second year he was $200 in debt.

In 1874 he took up a homestead and by dint of hard work and push, taking contracts for splitting rails, digging ditches, clearing lands, etc., etc., he wrested prosperity from adversity. He now has a commodious house, a fine grove of 1,400 trees, 200 bearing and 500 that will bear next year, and his place is valued at over $20,000. He also gives great attention to vegetable raising for market and finds ready sale. He has raised cattle, though he thinks the flat woods better for that business, owned and run a saw mill, built the Lucky House at Orlando (now the Charleston Hotel) which he still owns, and which is the most thoroughly constructed and finished building in this rapidly growing city. All this has not been accomplished without unexampled energy and a reputation for square and straightforward dealing, but it shows what can be done in this favored country.

REEL & FOSTER,

Livery, sale and feed stable. Also dealers in grain, hay and fertilizer. Corner Orange street and Central avenue, Orlando, Florida. This wide awake firm, E. J. Reel and P. A. Foster, have extensive new buildings, fine horses, new handsome and nobby turnouts, unexcelled in the State. Their charges are very reasonable and all their patrons are sure of courteous and gentlemanly treatment. Every few weeks they receive car loads of fine Kentucky horses for sale, thus giving the best of opportunities for securing an excellent team. Also wagons, buggies and carriages from the celebrated firm of S. B. & C. Hayes, Washington, Pa.

MANGOLD & SON.

PRACTICAL LANDSCAPE ARTISTS, PALATKA, FLA.

They have on hand the largest assortment of Florida views of any publishers in the State, their collection embracing nearly two hundred different views of Orange county alone, among which are views of orange groves in different stages, from that just planted to the grove in full bearing. Views of beautiful lakes, moss scenery, residences, villages, towns and cities; in fact almost everything of interest to be found in the State. For $1.50 they will mail to any address one dozen assorted views. Address,

MANGOLD & SON,
Palatka, Florida.

BUREAU OF FLORIDA INFORMATION.

Newspapers, Circulars, Pamphlets and reliable written information furnished on all matters pertaining to Florida, and especially as regards "The Orange Belt," in proportion to the amount of remittance. Address,

SHERMAN ADAMS,
Orlando, Fla.

MR. GEO. W. MOYERS.

Among the pioneers in the saw mill business in Orange county, may be mentioned Geo. W. Moyers, who came to this county in 1875 and engaged in the manufacture of lumber for building purposes. At that time it was considered by many as a hazardous enterprise, but by fair dealing with all and a close application to his business personally, he has won for himself the reputation of being the "Boss Saw Mill" man of the county, and the lumber manufactured by him always stands A 1 among the carpenters who have had access to his mill. Commencing with very limited capital he first began on Lake Orienta, near the present site of the fine Altamonte Hotel, operating there for one year and then moving to Lake Virginia, now the beautiful site of Winter Park, at which point he carried on his business for six years. During this time he met with many serious drawbacks well calculated to dishearten a more timid man; but with a firm faith in the rapid development of the county, and a determination not to be beaten in the race, he has during this year moved to a point on the west bank of the Wekiva river, three miles from the railroad at Snow's Station, (or Altamonte Hotel) and immediately on the line dividing the Altamonte settlement from Forest City—Orange Park. Here he has fitted up one of the most complete establishments in South Florida for the manufacture of building lumber, and is prepared now to supply complete bills of house lumber either rough or dressed, and, for quality of lumber and workmanship he challenges comparison with any mill in the county. In addition to his regular lumber trade he is putting in special machines for the manufacture of plaster laths, orange boxes, and vegetable crates, for which there will be a good demand in the near future. He is located in one of the finest timbered sections of the county, and in the midst of the grand boom now being enjoyed by Altamonte and Forest City, with a homestead of one hundred and sixty acres of splendid land he will soon reap some of the harvest for which he has been so long working.

Parties who contemplate building or using lumber for other purposes will do well to call at the "Boss Saw Mill," and Mr. Moyers will always be glad to make estimates for bills, and is prepared with ample teams to deliver lumber in any quantity and at any point within ten miles on very reasonable terms.

On his own place he has erected one of the best dwelling houses in the county, and has in grove about 500 orange trees, some of which are bearing one thousand oranges this season, on land where seven years ago the stately pine was king of the fields. So much for pluck and energy.

CAPT. T. J. SHINE'S
ABSTRACTS OF TITLES IN ORANGE COUNTY.

The above work is of great value to persons intending to purchase land, having been prepared by a great outlay of skill, time and expense. These huge volumes show at a glance the exact status of any piece of land in Orange county as to ownership, taxes, judgments, liens, etc., and can be relied upon as being correct in all particulars. Capt. Shine's official position and experience as Clerk of the Circuit Court gives him the best possible means of obtaining information on these points, and he has courteous and able assistants.

THE SANFORD JOURNAL.

A weekly newspaper published every Thursday at Sanford, Orange county, Florida. The Journal is devoted to the development of SOUTH FLORIDA, and heartily favors all proper schemes and enterprises whether undertaken by the State or individuals, which seek to induce immigration and development. It will encourage all industries which give promise of benefit, and will seek to furnish such reliable information as will be of value to the citizens, and to those desiring to become citizens.

The moral tone of the Journal will be such as to render it an acceptable visitor to the family circle, while in typographical execution it will be the equal of any paper in the State.

Sanford is the head of navigation of the St. Johns river for large steamers, is the northern terminus of two railroads, and the commercial center of a large and growing section of country. Its growth has been phenomenal, and its prospects of a large population and extensive business are flattering.

The subscription price of the Journal is $2.00 per year, payable invariably in advance.

J. J. HARRIS, Editor and Prop'r.

THE ORANGE COUNTY REPORTER.
MAHLON GORE, EDITOR.

A weekly, published at Orlando, Orange county, Florida, at $2.00 per year. Send five cents for sample copy.

BANK OF ORLANDO.

Prominent among the evidences of the rapid progress, growth and development of Orange county is the flourishing condition of the BANK OF ORLANDO. This financial institution, started almost as an experiment less than a year since, shows unexampled success as an investment, and has immeasurably aided all classes in their efforts to secure homes, develop business and make the wilderness blossom as the rose. Tourists, traders, land hunters and pleasure seekers, as well as men of business and other residents need only to produce proper letters of credit from other banks and their drafts will be cashed. Mr. Charles Joy, of Wells River, Vt., is the President, and Mr. Nat. Poyntz, a gentleman well known in Maysville, Ky., and also throughout the whole State of Florida, is the Cashier. So rapidly has the business of the Bank increased the present season that additional force was needed, and Mr. Wm. B. Newton, of Covington, Ky., has been elected assistant cashier, and Mr. W. N. Nall collecting clerk. Those having business with this institution are assured the most considerate attention possible.

J. K. DUKE & CO.

The gentlemen comprising this firm possess those peculiar social qualities and gentlemanly manners that endear them to all who once make their acquaintance, and by their business tact and careful regard for the wants of their customers they have established a business second to none in their line in South Florida. They have one of the most attractive business houses in Orlando, centrally located on the corner of Pine and Court Streets, and make first class goods and low prices a specialty. They are remarkably successful in meeting the wants of their customers, and those who trade with them once are sure to go again. They keep a full assortment of first-class staple and fancy groceries and provisions, their goods being unexcelled for quality. Among other things too numerous to mention, we note a full line of California canned goods. Mr. Duke came from Kentucky in 1878, started a store in 1880 and the present firm in 1882. He has a lovely home a little north of the court house with a great variety of fruits and flowers. He also owns lands and several fine groves out of the corporation limits.

BON AIR LUNG CURE.

For all lung and bronchial diseases, and kindred complaints arising therefrom. The multitudes of people now suffering with consumption, bronchitis, asthma, inflamation of the lungs or bronchial tubes, can find a cure. This new compound is composed of the most purifying and healing roots, gums and plants, grown in the fields and forests of Florida.

No one will doubt the efficacy of this remedy after a trial. Thousands have filled untimely graves for want of knowledge of proper treatment or through delay. The thief of life enters quietly and steals the noblest of our race. No matter how far advanced your case may be, TRY IT. If it is just creeping upon you, DO NOT DELAY.

For the protection of the public and the manufacturer each label will bear our trade mark. None is genuine without the map of Florida, on which is a shield bearing the words, "Trade Mark—Bon Air Health—50 cents, $1 and $2 per bottle." Ask your druggist to send for it. Address.

BON AIR LABORATORY,
Orlando, Fla.

SOUTH FLORIDA SADDLERY.

Harness, from the cheapest plow gear to the most stylish carriage harness. Saddles, all styles and prices, from $3 up. Bridles, collars, hames, leather oil, etc. Everything pertaining to horse and mule harness at manufacturers prices, for cash. Repairing promptly done. Factory and salesrooms opposite court house. Call on or address South Florida Saddlery, Orlando, Florida.

INTERIOR LAND AGENCY.

Office Orlando, Florida. Free teams convey land hunters over the different sections. Lands adapted to orange, lemon, pineapple, banana, and all semi-tropical fruit culture, as well as tobacco, cane, corn, and general truck gardening. Improved orange groves and wild land, select locations, high lake fronts, level lands or hills. The piney hills of the interior of South Florida are unquestionably the most healthful resort in the world for those afflicted with consumption, catarrh, asthma, or any bronchial affections, rheumatism and many other complaints, and can be reached at a comparatively trifling expense. Lands bought and sold on commission, land cleared, groves made and cultivated for non-residents. Call on or address with stamp,

INTERIOR LAND AGENCY.

www.ingramcontent.com/pod-product-compliance
Lightning Source LLC
Chambersburg PA
CBHW020859160426
43192CB00007B/990